JOURNAL OF SEMITIC STUDIES
MONOGRAPH No. 5

1948 AND AFTER:
ASPECTS OF
ISRAELI FICTION

BY

LEON I. YUDKIN

Lecturer in Modern Hebrew
University of Manchester

UNIVERSITY OF MANCHESTER 1984

BRITISH LIBRARY CATALOGUING IN PUBLICATION
DATA

Yudkin, Leon I.

1948 and after: aspects of Israeli fiction.—(Journal of semitic
studies monograph series, ISSN 0024-4480; no. 5)
1. Hebrew fiction—History and criticism
I. Title   II. Series
892.4'36'09   PJ5029

ISBN 0-9507885-1-1

Published by the University of Manchester

First published 1984

Printed in Belgium by the Imprimerie Orientaliste,
Louvain

CONTENTS

To Rebecca and Isaac Goss
who made this book possible

ACKNOWLEDGEMENTS

I would like to express my thanks to the University of Manchester for its generous aid towards visits to Israel, to my colleague M. E. J. Richardson for his advice in the preparation of this manuscript, and to I. Goldberg of the Institute for the Translation of Hebrew Literature in Tel-Aviv for his aid in the preparation of the English language bibliography.

Some of the material in this book appeared earlier in a rather different form in *Modern Hebrew Literature* and the *Journal of Semitic Studies*.

Thanks are due also to the Cultural Department of the Israeli Embassy in London, for some assistance in publication costs.

פתח דבר אל הקורא העברי

בזה אני מגיש לקורא האנגלי ספר המקיף קווים כלליים של הסיפורת הישראלית. כדי להגיש להגדרת הנושא שלי, הקדמת תיאור רקע לבירור הנושא היהודי בימינו ולמקומה של הספרות הישראלית בתמונה כולה. השרשים לסיפורת הישראלית מהם? האם ניתן לבודד תאריך גורלי כמו 1948 כמוקד גם לתולדות הספרות העברית? קומה של המדינה הוא נקודת מוצא של הספר מבחינה כרונולוגית, אך נחוץ גם לחשוף את שרשיה וניצניה של התקופה מקודם.

השתדלתי לשלב שני סוגי דיון בספר - דיון הסטורי מזה ודיון אסתטי מזה. עצם הדיון ההסטורי בספרות מצטדק על ידי מתן ערך לאמנות. משום כך, הפרקים כתובים מנקודות מבט שונות. לעתים הם עוסקים בסוגיה מסוימת, ולעתים בסופר מסוים (אם בסך כל יצירתו ואם בחתך מוגבל). עיקר מטרתי הוא להציג תמונה כוללת של התופעה כדי לעורר התעניינות בספרות הישראלית ובהערכתה.

תודתי נתונה לכל שהושיטו לי יד, אם במישרין ואם בעקיפין, בהכנת הספר.

ל. י.

PREFACE

The presentation of any history of literature is problematic. A total account is not inconceivable, but could be meaningless in its lack of selectivity. On the other hand, a selective account, the one that must be given, is necessarily partial and arbitrary.

The offering here neither pretends nor aspires to completeness. These aspects of Israeli fiction could be amplified in many directions. In this presentation I have tried to combine two methods within the framework of a single volume. The first method is the overall characterisation of a particular author, his modes, his concerns, his ambitions and his achievements. Sometimes, within this purview, I have presented not a total chronology, but either a partial one, such as a specific part of an author's opus, or an analysis of a particular piece of writing. The second method is the attempted characterisation of a group of writers which, for example, belong to a given period, or of a particular problem, such as the way a novel ends. I have also considered the total extent of language registers in Hebrew, the overall perspective in Hebrew writing as such, and types of experimentation within the literature. Some may argue that the two sorts of presentation do not marry naturally. I have, however, taken the view that the two approaches must be balanced simultaneously; specific focus on a given opus and the larger context within which that opus has arisen. So this is a study both of 'trends' and of 'writers'.

Another problem is the apparent arbitrariness of periodisation and choice of material. The period selected for discussion within Hebrew fiction is that of the State of Israel, 1948 and onwards. Naturally there are some writers who began their narrative activity long before then and continued afterwards; their pre-State work is included because they also figure prominently in the period of the State. This is an attempt to portray Israeli fiction, with some of its pre-1948 antecedents.

The literary critical method adopted here is to attempt to grasp the central features of the writing described, to characterise and analyse it, to try to view its ambitions and to mark out its achievements. No one focus has therefore been imposed on the writing, since, of course, writers have different foci, ambitions and problems. To expect the same thing from disparate materials would be absurd. But there are common problems, such as the use of the same language, the operation within one social and political context, and a particular historical situation. I have tried to note both the common and the divergent.

In earlier work I have attempted an overall sketch of Israeli literature, and I am not intending to duplicate material in my *Escape Into Siege* (1974), which this book, to some extent, supplements. But the concentration here is on a single genre.

My indebtedness to other writers, critics and teachers is too extensive to itemise in detail. But it is evident in every page, either directly or indirectly. My thanks go out to all of them.

I have tried to provide literal English translations of the titles of those works not yet published in English and approximate transliterations for the benefit of those readers who know no Hebrew.

HEBREW LITERATURE TODAY:
JEWISH WORLD OR ISRAELI PROVINCE?

At about the time of the emergence of Israeli independence, a perceptible sense of the new Israeli separatism was being expressed in various forms. An editorial statement in the periodical אלף *Alef* (June 1951) records: 'Neither are the Jews a homogeneous people; nearly half are of Asian or African stock, and are totally different from Europeans. But today the principal distinction is not between the various traditional communities within Jewry, but between all these and the increasing number of Israeli youth, embodied in the type of the Sabra, the Israeli-born youth, who is particularly non-Jewish in appearance, outlook and horizons'. Here the fact of the Sabra is asserted, as is his separateness and autonomy. The Israeli is set on the stage, a created fiction more than an inescapably historical fact. Essential to the new Israel was the new Israeli man. The Israeli novelist Benjamin Tammuz puts the ideology in the mouth of his eponymous hero Jacob, recalling his youth in the 40s; 'He was not born here ... the people who said this were also not born here. Not one of the members of the underground was born here. But they all believed that they had shaken off the heritage of their Jewish extraction and were altogether Hebrews'.[1] This sort of Hebraism (the group was also sometimes known as the Young Hebrews) or Canaanism, as it was popularly styled, did not merely recognise the geographic divide between the Jews of Palestine/Israel and the Diaspora, but further posited an ideological divide and a different breed of person. This stage was the culmination of several decades of the individual's perceived alienation from the mass of Jewry. But whereas it might earlier have taken the form of a lonely intellectual sense of rootlessness, isolation, unfulfilled social longing and frustration, it here seeks to establish a rootedness in the Land of Israel. To sharpen his declared identity, he proclaims his distinction through all available markings—geographical, linguistic, social and historical. The new historical attachment is staked to a more-

---

[1] In יעקב *Ya'aqov* (Jacob, 1971).

distant existence, as Jacob says later, reflecting on the War of Independence: 'Then through the struggle, I felt that I was coming into contact, deep and mysterious contact, with my national past'.

This extreme ideology of breach postulates a link with Biblical Israel and the contemporary Middle East. Sympathy is with that of language, location and a local Fate, not with that mysterious and foreign entity known as diaspora Jewry. Such a notion is the logical outcome of the ultimate denial of Exile required by a version of Zionism dialectically seeking to undermine and transform the condition of the Jew. Although Canaanism as such was a fringe movement, its associated attitudes were very prevalent in Israeli politics and literature. Ben-Gurion, for example, was explicitly uncomprehending of diaspora Jewish attitudes and of the refusal of Jews to move to Israel. The alternatives in contemporary Jewish life were presented to him quite starkly. But in leterature, too, the Sabra seemed to be living in a world remote from diaspora Jewish existence. S. Yizhar (born 1916) cultivates a new Hebrew writing with a rich, local syntax and vocabulary, rooted in Palestinian conditions, landscape and people. In the story חרבת חזעה *Hirbeth Hizah*,[2] the narrator (a participant in the action of the story which turns on the capture of an Arab village and the evacuation of its inhabitants) reflects that he had not understood the central feature of Jewish history until this moment—that of exile. And he can only understand it now because he sees an actual taking place, although in this case it is an exile brought about by the Jews rather than suffered by them. The distancing from Jewish history can only be eradicated by Biblical parallels; the intervening nineteen hundred years of post-Biblical Jewish history and diaspora existence have no tangible reality and can only be remotely sensed by implication or analogy. For all the criticism of majority action uttered or suggested by the narrative voice or the general voice of conscience in Yizhar's stories, the author still adopts a distinctly Sabra stance in a specifically Israeli world far removed from that other Jewish world on the periphery.

* * *

[2] In the volume ארבעה סיפורים *Arba'ah sipurim* (Four Stories, 1950).

It was not always thus. The modern Hebrew writer may not have been deeply attached to all aspects of Jewish life, but he had been shaped by it and was representative of it to some extent. The fact of being a writer cast him in a necessarily minority role. Hebrew writing was a minority activity and secular Hebrew writing was a rebellious practice. The Haskalah (Hebrew Enlightenment) had adopted Hebrew literature as a programme of change and reform. Perspectives were to be modified and life-patterns altered. The hero of the fin-de-siècle Hebrew story moves from the centre of Jewish life to the periphery, where he very often ponders Jewish fate (frequently his own) in very radical terms. We see that more often than not the writer is the hero in his own created world. Narrative reflections then closely approach the authorial stance on questions discussed. A major preoccupation of M. Y. Berdyczewski (1865-1921) is that of a 'transvaluation of values', a Nietzschean term conscripted into a Jewish context. But this transvaluation is not of an abstract, theoretical kind directed at the people in general. In this sense, he differs from his adversary Ahad Ha'am (1856-1927) who does seem to display an Olympian attachment in his speculations on the nature of Judaism and the possibilities of its renaissance. But Berdyczewski obtrudes his own personal concerns, both into his stories and into his essays. His typical fictional hero is the young Jew on his way 'out of the ghetto' into Europe. Since he belongs to neither world completely, he is a type of the marginal man nowhere totally at home, but with great aspirations to reform. It has been noted that the fascination of the outer, gentile world is paralleled by his attraction to the healthy, gentile woman. In the story appropriately entitled מחניים *Mahanayim* (Two Camps), the young student, entranced by the lovely, gentile lady, ponders the situation of his people and execrates its condition and dilatoriness; 'But why do not the sons of Jacob break all the cords at once? Why do they not open the windows, and instead close them'? The windows, of course, let in the light and the air of the outside world. And the Jews (in this image) fear the wind of change that would blow in with these no doubt desirable and fascinating entities. H. N. Bialik (1865-1934) too has used the window image to illustrate the same situation, featuring it as a phenomenon both attractive and dangerous. But the Berdyczewski hero has not the doubts of the poet in his attempt to grasp the seductive object. Here are the reflections of the hero at the opening of

מחניים *Mahanayim*; 'Earlier, he had been exclusively in the line of his ancestor's inheritance, and had guarded those ancestral traditions. Now he had wandered beyond their range and was labouring to nullify everything acquired between the walls. He had left darkness for light, servitude for freedom; and this free man was living in some poor, obscure corner, with little to eat and with many books'. Our hero has various of the attributes of traditional heroism—soaring ambition, youth, potential. But his typology is characteristic of writers of the period. The old world of Judaism is to be jettisoned as a dark province, and he is excited by the prospect of the 'light'. He would step out to conquer the new, 'external' world, although he may take some part of his Hebrew baggage with him, suitably adapted to modern circumstance. Berdyczewski was a fictionalist and a rebel, a Hebraist who asserted that there was always another stream alongside mainstream Judaism, sometimes running counter to it. He found in Nietzsche's anti-Christianity a model for his anti-mainstream Judaism, and like other Hebrew writers, such as S. Tschernichovsky (1875-1943) he conducted a virile opposition to what he regarded as the subjugated, passive world of the ghetto—a vitalism of Art and Eros. He was strongly opposed to the traditionalism of Ahad Ha'am, a traditionalism by no means allied to Jewish orthodoxy or textual fundamentalism, but that is rather a positivist reading of historical Judaism with the supernatural element removed. Ahad Ha'am saw himself as a defender and reviver of the tradition. He sought to revive the Hebrew language too and restore its rightful place as the centre of the Jewish world as the instrument of its chief expression. It was the national Jewish language. Whereas, for example, Aramaic, Ladino and Yiddish were languages that Jews used to a greater or lesser extent, Hebrew was the only language that was truly national even if spoken by almost no-one and used as a means of literary communication by the very few. It was, however, historically and geographically at the centre of Jewish experience, the medium of the central (and sanctified) texts. It was not associated with any one community or single epoch, but was the kernel of the total Jewish experience. He strenuously argued not only against the assimilationists but also against Jewish educationists who did not recognise the centrality of Hebrew. In such a polemic (an essay entitled 'National Education' 1902) he writes: '... the national element stands out in the teaching of

4

geography and history, but beyond all national educational tools especially outstanding is the teaching of the national language and its literature'. Language permeates and creates the child's world, bolsters and integrates his conceptual framework so that he sees everything in terms of that language. This is nothing to do with chauvinism but is simply what 'the nation' consists of. If you merely learn about your culture in the language of the State (i.e. not in Hebrew) you will be approaching it as a foreigner and will therefore remain outside. You will lack the inwardness and integration of the national, the member of the family who is part of that family for good or evil, not because that family is better, but simply because it is yours. The language creates your world and interprets other worlds for you! The Hebrew Jew will not be a Jew split into two elements —'man' (general) and 'Jew' (specific), an unsatisfactory hydra— but rather an integrated, total and national human being/Jew. Ahad Ha'am wrote mainly in the Hebrew that was undergoing a revival that he was supporting so much by various means. And although this language was the minority concern, this minority purported to speak for the nation at large, as well as for the State on the way. The Hebrew author saw the national language as the instrument with which to establish an organic wholeness amongst a Jewish people losing adherents through depredation, persecution, assimilation, loss of religious faith and lack of national direction. The late nineteenth century was not a high point of international Jewish fortune. But the growth of the national movement offered a new focus and lease of life to a waning sense of identity.

A different aspect of the national renaissance was presented by Y. H. Brenner (1881-1921), a Hebrew writer excluded by Ahad Ha'am in his capacity as editor of the journal *Hashiloah*. Brenner was also much involved with the Hebrew revival, but he always qualified this involvement with the caution that the dimensions of this revival were far short of that greater European renaissance. He regarded the Jewish situation as pathological, requiring radical treatment that would leave the patient healthier but still fairly insignificant. He placed great stress on social corrective; on economic self-reform, on self-labour and on return to the soil (of Palestine). He abhorred abstractions, particularly theoretical notions of 'culture', certainly of Jewish culture, outside of its social and economic context. Any national revival would first of all require a revolutionised infra-structure. All theory and abstraction were for him an abrogation of the truth. Fiction was not merely something illustrative, but rather, insofar as it recreated the individual's particular circumstances and conflict, the heart of the matter. The Jewish situation was the situation of the specific Jew himself and others known personally. That Jew was suffering, his condition was miserable, and the means required to etch such a condition had to match up aesthetically. Not with fine form and polished sentences, but with tools equivalent to the described condition. So he produced a rough-hewn prose, reflecting the mind of the individual conjured up, heated, yearning, striving, frustrated and perhaps, sick. Such a type is Yehezkel Hefetz, a mental patient in Jerusalem, of שכול וכשלון (1920)[3] written over the course of the last years of Brenner's life spent in Palestine. As a type of Hebrew spokesman of the day, Hefetz was the complete antithesis of 'national hero'—ugly, unsuccessful, improverished, ungraceful. But in this character the author invested his major labour, building up a picture of degredation and disappointment that could, at the most, be modified by personal devotion and self-sacrifice. Hefetz (appropriately meaning 'desire') embodies the total local situation, a situation that is also the apex of the 'renaissance', the condition of the yishuv. Hefetz was of the type already familiar to fin-de-siècle Hebrew fiction—unrooted, marginal, impoverished, dislocated. He is the type who had lost out on the old and was on his way to the new cultures. But he was not just in search of national fulfilment, but of himself too, of a true identity that could link truly to others, that would feel honestly and attain his own fulfilment, however unspectacular. Hefetz is accused by his friend of existing in isolation, unrelated to external reality. He has to be extended. So for all his exposure to the truth of his own condition he is still not genuinely in touch with anything beyond himself. Perhaps that is the nature of his sickness.

We can see then different faces of the Hebrew spokesman of the Jewish condition. There is the language as the tool of national restoration, the key to the lock of history and national tradition. Or there is the expression of the anguished individual in a frenzied effort to re-establish his roots, perhaps in a different context. Or, it is the representative of that other line of the Jewish heritage, repressed and rejected. In any case, it

[3] Translated as *Breakdown and Bereavement* (Tel Aviv, 1971).

is a messenger to the Jewish people; to the whole people potentially, if only to a few in actual practice. The Hebrew writer was integrally linked to the fortunes of his nation in his programme and his craft.

* * *

This observation of the Hebrew writer addressing the people as a whole holds good for Hebrew literature throughout the ages. Clearly after the unification of the tribes before the dispersion, the Biblical nation was viewed as one. This is so even after the fall of the Northern Kingdom and that irremediable split. But in the diaspora too, the Jews were perceived as a single people, of one God, History and Fate; certainly the Hebrew writer posited that assumption, and his linguistic vehicle supported this notion. The introduction of printing facilitated communication and made the assumption practicable. In modern times, in the post-Emancipation phase, the Jews were divided into separate national entities, and individuals were invited to identify with the political entity (Nation-State) in which they resided. A new loyalty competed. Now there was not the pre-eminent division of the world into Empires or religious groupings. Particularly from the late eighteenth century onwards the Jew became a national citizen (citoyen), and was sometimes made to feel that a sense of Jewish loyalty, if it were a national loyalty, was incompatible with a specific political loyalty. And the bearers of the message of Emancipation had to propagate this exchange of loyalties. After all, they were seeking entry into European civilisation, so they had to pay a political price. The price of Joseph II's 'Toleranz-Edikt' (1781), of the French declaration of the 'Droits de l'Homme (1789) and of the Soviet revolutionary promulgation of personal equality (1917) was an abandonment of local and contradictory attachments. The maskilim (enlighteners) sometimes co-operated with the sense of the demand. N. H. Wessely (1725-1805) in his pamphlet דברי שלום ואמת 'Words of Peace and Truth' (1782) welcomed the prospect of superior education, and suggested that the Jews should take advantage of the extended offer, to broaden horizens and participate in a great experience. M. Mendelssohn (1729-1786) not only shared the sentiments of this Movement but was actually its precursor in his life and work. He wanted the Jews of Germany to be free to participate in the larger society as was he himself, and so he requested both

7

modification of credal demands made by Christians on the one hand, and of separatism on the part of the Jews, on the other. Indeed, in Germany we find that both cultural and religious assimilation proceeded apace in the succeeding century, to such a degree, in fact, that Samson Raphael Hirsch (1808-1888) had difficulty in locating human material for the Orthodox community that he was to establish in Frankfurt in 1851. Meanwhile, the Hebrew Enlightenment had virtually disappeared in Germany, melting into a German context, and sometimes accompanied by religious conversion.

But this fissiparous tendency was that of the 'Enlightenment', which soon adopted the guise of specific political loyalty to the host nation. The Hebrew writer, as such, addressed the general Jewish public, and only ceased to do so when he stopped writing Hebrew. Mendelssohn's adoption of German is not so much a cause of assimilation as a symptom of it. Hebrew had been a stepping stone from Yiddish to German. But now, the author was not so much addressing the Jew as he was addressing the German reader in general, and the Jew incidentally. As a Hebrew writer, Mendelssohn had offered a programme—a philosophical, religious and educational approach. As a Hebrew writer, he had addressed the Jewish people as had earlier Hebrew writers. Of course, segmentation was beginning to set in. But then he ceased to function as a Hebrew writer.

In Eastern Europe, such segmentation could not take place so easily. The Jewish community still existed strongly during 'Enlightenment' times. It even grew stronger in the course of the nineteenth century with the dramatic rise of (particularly Jewish) population, and its confinement within the Pale of Settlement. Not until the mass emigrations following the 1881 pogroms was there to be a serious dent in the Community or in its organisational and social structures. Whatever the conditions (and, of course, those were tough) there was a recognisable Nation within the State, with some of the instruments of nationhood-communal organisation, a language and, thus too, a literature. So the East European Enlightenment writer continued, after the promulgation of his programme, to address the Jews as a Nation. Whereas Mendelssohn changed his language and, hence, his readership, Mendeli Mocher Sforim (1836-1917), for example, exchanged *a* national language for *the* national language. He had been a Hebrew writer of the

8

Enlightment type, turned to Yiddish in search of a more popular medium of expression, but then went back to Hebrew, a Hebrew now vitalised and reformed, not exclusively Biblical, to cast his earlier Yiddish material in a tongue that he assumed would live as long as the Jews. So he accepts the more restricted readership and the difficulties inherent in writing a language that was not a vernacular in return for the possibly larger gains of the permanent Hebrew heritage. Of course, he still offered a programme. Such was always the nature of the Hebrew writer who did not inhabit a belle lettristic vacuum, but occupied a central role as a Jewish 'intelligent'. Particularly was this the case in Eastern Europe, where the writer in the main is not a marginal figure of fun, but an involved participant and reformer, bringing the truth to the people and a message for those who would hear it. In his early phase, Mendeli was a representative 'enlightener' promoting the virtues of education. And in his later phase, when he created literature of a much higher order, his satire became sharper and his pathos deeper. His capacity grew with the increased sophistication of his literary instrument, so that he could indeed father a new literature. Brenner saw him in his well-known essay הערכה עצמית בשלשת הכרכים 'Self-estimation in the Three Volumes' (1914) as the first to expose the true (and indeed disgraceful) condition of the people. Brenner reads Mendeli as a Brennerist, castigating the people for their parasitic condition. Education cannot be bought in a void, without social change, without indeed social revolution. You cannot change the surface epi-phenomenon without transforming the soil whence it emanates. In Brenner's view, Mendeli drew the condition of the Jews mercilessly and precisely in attacking his merely marginal involvement in society, his involvement to the extent of deriving the benefit without contribution to its creation. Brenner's is a partisan interpretation, a brilliant conscription of his older contemporary to his cause. And we do not at this moment have to decide whether his interpretation is wholly just or not. But what we can perceive from the shape of nineteenth-century Hebrew fiction, is a movement from a moderate and optimistic programme of reform to an outright demand for revolution. Also, from a concern with types, with the general and the characteristic, kindly ironic or satirical, to a more overwhelming concern with the psychology of the individual. But throughout, in all phases of this Hebrew writing (because

9

this applies in large measure to the poetry too, even to lyric poetry), the writer sets himself in the Jewish world, to describe it, to castigate it maybe, but certainly to address it.

* *

The real divide between the Jewish world and the Israeli province comes at a later stage. The Hebrew writer, insofar as he remained such, was largely involved in the Jewish reality, up to and through the First World War. At about that time, certain events began to confirm pre-existent trends that were then to solidify further. One was the breakdown of the Jewish community in the Russian Pale. The victorious Bolsheviks technically obliterated the limitations of the Pale and confirmed the doctrines of the French Revolution in their own territory. But of course, there the alternatives presented to the Jews were much more radical. They were not only (by implication) asked to surrender national, cultural expression for full rights (such as they were) but were also negatively singled out in comparison to other 'nationalities' and were to suffer particularly in the purges. Community life disappeared, the use of Yiddish was reduced and brought under State control and Hebrew was forbidden (although there persisted a trickle of underground writing). In the other large diaspora, in the USA, the natural effect of a plural, open society was to reduce separate cultural or linguistic expression. The Jews not only reaped the full benefits of a flourishing and affluent democracy and were quickly acculturated and anglicised, they also, in many cases, followed the predominant tendency and asserted the 'melting pot' view of nationalities within the State. So the two leading Jewish communities were fast disappearing as cultural enclaves in which Jewish literature (in its own languages) could flourish. This was to effect the virtual demise of Hebrew in the diaspora, as the pattern of these two communities was to be repeated elsewhere, in one or other of the versions presented.

On the other hand, Palestine from this time on was to become the natural focus of Hebrew activity. From the Balfour Declaration onwards, the third aliyah more than doubled the existing settlement. For the first time, too, the actual instruments of autonomy were forged, politically, socially and militarily. The Jewish community in Palestine began to look like the State on the way. Many of the Hebrew writers naturally committed to Jewish civilisation moved during this time to Palestine (both for negative reasons—the decline of Jewish life in the diaspora, and for positive reasons——the rise of Jewish Palestine). For example, Brenner moved in 1909, Ahad Ha'am in 1921, Bialik in 1924. This was the generation of the Hebrew cultural revivalists which had already grown to maturity. With conditions trans formed so dramatically, no further generation of Hebrew writers was to emerge with quite that sort of cultural baggage, the product of a particular Jewish environment. It was all to change in this respect. But not in all other respects. In spite of the events of the 30s and 40s, these decades merely confirmed existing patterns as far as the course of current Hebrew literature was concerned. The diaspora became weaker, Jewish Palestine stronger, and this polarisation has had effects which are still with us. This tendency, rather than suffer any reverse, has even threatened to become total.

The results are known. Palestine was to become the virtually sole venue of Hebrew activity, not just the centre with the diaspora as periphery in the terms of Ahad Ha'am. However, Ahad Ha'am's advocacy and prophecy were not completely falsified. For Eretz Yisrael was still a focus for diaspora Jewry in various senses. Physically it represented a refuge, 'spiritually' it provided a focal point for diaspora Jewry in many of its political, social and cultural activities. Culturally, the diaspora remains separate from Israel for two reasons. Culture is so rooted in local conditions, geographical, social and linguistic. A literature clearly emerges from local soil and from the language spoken and used, so it is inevitable that in the increasingly monolingual and monocultural situations of modern states, Hebrew is almost bound to take a back seat. But the second reason is that the trend of events set in earlier times has been reinforced, though with significant divergences and inter-ruptions. The decline of religion as a all-embracing force has inevitably displaced religious civilisation with a secular counterpart composed of either plural or alternative elements. And social pluralism has reversed the separateness of peoples within a state. This applies specifically and considerably to the Jews who are fully integrated into modern life the world over.

It has been said that there are three great events peculiar to modern Jewish history; the Emancipation, the Holocaust and the creation of the Israeli State. No one of these things took place just at one time, or once and for all. They are also historically and dialectically related. The Emancipation was set in motion by host nations which brought the Jews into the body politic. The Holocaust represents the most extreme rejection of the Jews by those nations which either explicitly or implicitly did not want to bring the Jews in; perhaps the Emancipation was qualified anyway. Also, the State of Israel is the ultimate response on the part of the Jews who either sensed that rejection or who did not specifically seek acceptance. Zionism is an assertion of national identity unimaginable outside the context of the general rise of nationalism in the nineteenth century, but nevertheless constituting a particularly Jewish response. Certainly, in physical terms, these three linked events can usefully illuminate the position of Hebrew letters in the world today.

* *

Now virtually half the Jews in the world live in the USA, to some extent organised in sub-movements of religious affiliation. They display considerable interest in and loyalty to Israel, as evidenced by fund-raising, political activities and educational bias. But, as Mordechai Kaplan has argued[4], there has not developed a distinctly American Zionism appropriate to American conditions. Kaplan rejects the notion that Judaism is exclusively or even primarily theological, powered by religious doctrine. Even though in the USA the Jews do not now live in a defined area, do not speak their own language, do not operate their own law, nevertheless they still retain some national elements which might be strengthened, and they do focus on Israel. Thus Kaplan attempts to adapt Ahad Ha'amism to American conditions.

American views of Judaism can be divided, following Arthur Cohen's terminology, into the Natural and the Supernatural.[5] The Natural view sees Jews functioning in the world as one people amongst many, sharing the normal historical phenomenology and subject to the recognisable operation of life as with other peoples. In contemporary life they inhabit the 'secular city' which has reduced the place of God in the world. Richard Rubenstein is in the Pragmatist-Reconstructionist tradition, and takes up Harvey Cox's view of contemporary life—though

[4] See *A new Zionism* (New York, 1955).
[5] Arthur Cohen, *The natural and the supernatural Jew* (New York, 1962).

without the optimism. From *After Auschwitz*[6] he puts the Holocaust at the centre of the contemporary situation. Genocide, the total abandonment of any vestige of morality, has confirmed the death of God. But here too Rubenstein adopts the Naturalist viewpoint and is very concerned to place even the events of the Second World War in the context of normative history. In *The cunning of history*[7] the Holocaust is seen as the culmination of technocratic society, a total form of enslavement and the ultimate in secularity. It has confirmed the need to jettison the notion of 'chosenness' which today has taken on a nasty, sick irony. Like the Naturalists, he wants the Jews to play on the stage of History as just one of the many actors, like any other people. And for him, the State of Israel bolsters the people's normality.

The other view presents Jewish history as being something specific and peculiar, deriving from a peculiar relationship with God. For A. J. Heschel, the central realisation is the appreciation of the 'ineffable', that quality that is precisely beyond human containment.[8] This, for him, is what the Jewish tradition celebrates. It is something special, too, for Will Herberg in *Judaism and modern man*[9] where a unique place is carved out for Judaism in its dialectic with other cultures. Judaism is thus a source of truth in absolute terms and not just one of several civilisations. And Emil Fackenheim in his consideration of the Holocaust takes it as a Jewish phenomenon within Jewish history.[10] This view argues that the Holocaust was not a casual event that could have occurred anywhere with anyone, but one that specifically related to Jews. Rubenstein rejects the notion of martyrdom as inapplicable here, arguing that those who were sent to their deaths exercised no freedom of choice. But Fackenheim sees the Jewish Fate as one elected. Had the grandparents of those murdered rejected their Jewishness, the grandchildren would not have gone. And their reaction to the Holocaust in persisting in their Jewishness still affirms that fate. Jews, as a people, have deliberately embraced their persistent character.

[6] Indianapolis, 1966.
[7] New York, 1975.
[8] *God in search of man* (New York, 1955).
[9] New York, 1951.
[10] See for example *God's presence in history* (New York, 1971) and *The Jewish return into history* (New York, 1978).

13

This debate turns on the nature of Jewishness, the possibility of community and the notion of Jewish history. In the purely physical sense, there has naturally taken place a slackening in the tightness of that community (if we can now speak at all of a community in any single sense); domestic conditions have spread the Jews throughout the country and absorbed them into Americanism. In their literature too, Jewish writers have not been writing exclusively for Jews in Jewish languages. There was a natural move from Jewish writing to writing about Jews for the general reader. Yiddish writers turned to English as did that doyen of early American Yiddishists, Abraham Cahan, whose major novel *The rise of David Levinsky* [11] was composed in English. Nevertheless, both Jewish subject matter and Yiddish echoes are retained in English language works. Henry Roth's fine (and only) novel *Call it sleep* [12] is written in a deliberately 'translated' tongue, with Yiddishisms and accents preserved in the speech patterns of the immigrant characters. And this attempt to capture a particular Jewish flavour is made in the post-war generation too, by writers as diverse as Bernard Malamud whose characters are often immigrants themselves, and Philip Roth who tries to present specifically American-Jewish types in an over-protective mother and aspirant, rebellious son. In a different way, Saul Bellow has recognisably Jewish characters, restless, searching, intellectually curious but uncertain and despairingly articulate. Herzog and Sammler are such. But it is not only the figures in the novels and the language that they speak. There is in some sense a Jewish literature as a recognisable category of its own, rising beyond the mere fact of Jewish authorship.

However, there is no doubt that for Jewish literature to flourish as an entity, it has to be set within the context of a community. Clearly, there is no large function for a Jewish language in the USA outside the orbit of English. Contemporary Yiddish writers sprang ready-formed from another milieu. But within the larger American society, Jews have made tentative moves towards a sense of a group, towards being a viable community'. [13] Not all the elements want to be boiled down in the 'melting pot'. Interestingly enough, against all

[11] New York, 1917.
[12] New York, 1934.
[13] See *The new Jews* (New York, 1971).

odds, Soviet Jews too began to grope towards their limited 'Jewish National Movement' in the 1960s. So, in both, extreme versions of society as expressed politically, Jews have again been moving towards national or communal association. Some, it seems, are not content to see themselves merely as individuals, Jewish or otherwise. The surprising discovery had been made much earlier by Norman Podhoretz as he records in *Making it* [14] that America is not culturally neutral, allowing each element full free expression, and merely holding the ring. There is a WASP pressure from without. Perhaps no society can in fact be neutral and not all ethnicities will disappear as predicted by Will Herberg in *Protestant, Catholic, Jew.* [15] Now Jews are seeking out not only a community but a means of specific Jewish expression. Cynthia Ozick, in her preface to a group of novellas, *Bloodshed* [16] says 'Since the coming forth from Egypt five millenia ago, mine is the first generation to think and speak wholly in English'. As English is a new medium for the Jewish writer, it cannot possibly express the range of historical and cultural association required. She would like a Jewish language, though, of course, it has to be contained now in her native English. Other Jewish writers have also sensed this need. They are looking for a specific cultural medium that would allow them to operate in a diaspora milieu and still be true to their specific vocation.

*   *
*

In consideration of how contemporary Hebrew literature confronts the totality of the Jewish people, we must bear two facts in mind. First, Hebrew literature is now almost exclusively written in Israel, and second, that the generations of writers who were nurtured on the soil of a partially autonomous (or quasi-autonomous) diaspora have almost entirely gone. It then follows that Hebrew literature today either relates primarily to the Israeli experience or to diaspora on the wane through destruction or assimilation. The last decade or so has witnessed the deaths of Burla, Hazaz, Shlonsky, Goldberg, Altermann, Kurzweil and Greenberg. Almost no one remains to provide the link with that other Jewish world.

[14] New York, 1968.
[15] New York, 1955.
[16] *Bloodshed and three novellas* (New York, 1976).

Israeli literature has, naturally enough, not been of one shade reflecting as it does the multifarious backgrounds of Israeli society, the different historical phases of its population and the literary influences and inclinations of its practitioners. But there have been certain predominant trends. At the time of the emergence of statehood, there was manifested extreme concern on the part of its writers for the character of that State, in respect to Israeli society, the war, the Kibbutz, absorption of immigrants and the new Israel. But from the 60s onwards, writers often reacted against the imposition of social expectations, and both in their introverted lyric poetry and in their fiction, they drew a strong inner world shielded from the public life of the State. In language too, the Israeli writer, particularly the poet, posed a counter-language to the high rhetoric of pre-State literature. Such poetry was often understated and slangy, seeking and capturing the rhythms of Israeli speech (for the first time in millennia, the Hebrew writer was writing the language spoken) in place of literary pastiche and learned allusion. But there has also been a return to the public, Jewish theme. S. Y. Agnon (1888-1971) could always remind us of the diaspora and Jewish history. Amongst the younger generation, A. Appelfeld (born 1932) from Bukovina, experiencing the war in Europe, has opted to write more about that other world. Both these writers have set stories in Europe, with the main figure returning there from Palestine/Israel on a visit. The universe of decayed or (with Appelfeld) dead Jewish Europe is thus seen through the lens of the latest phase of Jewish history. The dream of Zionism has to that degree been fulfilled. More recently, Israeli wars and the general situation of Israel have confirmed that the Jewish issue has not gone away. Israel is still not quite an ordinary State and the position of the Jew has not been completely normalised. So the Israeli phase is perceived by some writers as a phase of Jewish history for the Jewish people, and not as the 'end of the Jewish people' (George Friedmann's title posed as a question).[17] As popular as any theme is that of the Aqedah, the binding of Isaac and the attempted sacrifice by his father Abraham. As the first Jew had his faith tested by being commanded to surrender what was dearest to him, so the contemporary Jew is still so persuaded. Isaac the son is still the. offering for slaughter. Here, only too often, no angel intervenes

17 *Fin du peuple juif?* (Paris, 1965).

to hold back the sacrificial knife. Contemporary Hebrew literature seems once more set on the world Jewish stage.

Certainly the Hebrew writer of the fin-de-siècle addressed, (in theory at least) the whole Jewish world, and he addressed it as a finely tuned instrument, also representing it. The contemporary Hebrew writer does not do this in the same sense. The Jewish world is too refracted. Most of it is monolingual and mono-cultural, without deep roots in or links with the past. At least, these roots have not easily brought forth branches and fruit. The tools are broken. It is true too that the Jewish world is largely fractured, split into its separate communities of very widely varying fortunes and experiences. But on the other hand, even if there is no longer such a thing as a unitary Jewish culture, there is still an aspirant Jewish culture, with Hebrew as its subject and object. There is still too an historical experience even if it is an acquired and learned one. We have seen that the diaspora as well attends community and awaits the word. We have seen that the Israeli writer has been made part of the Jewish scene, even if that scene has not been an adopted option but, rather, one forced on him. And if Israel is in some sense the focus of contemporary Jewish experience, so too does Hebrew literature reflect and articulate that experience. Naturally, the quality of that reflection is of prime significance. But, in any case, Hebrew literature is still today of the Jewish world.

Every word in every language is loaded—that is, it contains an inner core belonging to historical usage and to the process of individual development. Every combination of words is loaded to a much greater extent, not only because of the plurality of elements in the combination but also because a combination by its very nature involves an added dimension. Any combination of words that does not lend itself to a faithful translation, that is, that does not preserve its particular original nuance in the language into which it is translated (the target language) is known as an idiom. The existence of the idiom points to the difficulty of translation of an extreme level and impresses upon us the hopelessness of precise transference from one language to another. But the problem exists at every linguistic level; it is inherent in the very phenomenon of the existence of different languages. How is one to understand fully the particular thought expressed, whether in speech or writing, without being aware of the fluctuations in meaning in the course of development of the language, the linguistic and cultural associations of the words expressed and the particular sense that the combination of words acquires according to linguistic and cultural conditions? Every language develops in its own direction and there is apparently no possibility of preserving the original nature of the source language in the target language. In considering this, Walter Benjamin came to the conclusion that if the translator seeks to transfer concepts of any kind from one language to another (and this after all is the translator's business and the justification of his efforts) he must constantly draw the reader's attention to the source language. A translator of this kind will create a new language to suit the demands of the original translated and its particular style; the original takes on a kind of sacrosanct nature and its primary shapes will be discernible even in foreign guise. It is the target language that changes, not the source. Thus, Benjamin took as his ideal example the translations of Scripture which sought (through feelings of admiration and reverence) to preserve the form of the original to an extreme degree, not to tamper with it, not even to adapt it, and went so far as to insert the source language between the lines of the translation and thus to re-create the style of the target language according to this pattern. His dictum, in the essay 'Die Aufgabe dieses Übersetzers' is expressed as: 'Die interlinear Version des Heiligen Textes ist das Urbild oder ideal aller Übersetzung'.[1]

But in fact, the average translator does not, in general, treat a literary work as if it were sacred, and he tries to devise for himself a means of preserving a measure of fidelity to the original, whilst preserving the evolved nature of the target language. Thus the reader of the target language will be able to enjoy the translation without undue effort, and at times, without even being conscious that the material is translated at all. There are some who seek to erase from their translations all trace of foreignness, so as to present the reader with familiar material and to absorb the foreign original to the extent that the absorption will not be perceived.

There are two ways of approaching the task: to preserve deliberately the feeling of foreignness so as to retain the spirit of the original, or to depart from the original to the extent that the need arises to find an appropriate model in the target language. But there is no avoiding the difficulty that the definitions and nomenclature of things present us with. What is fidelity? Is the attempt at literal translation tendentious? For, if so, that which was accepted or prevalent in the source language may become an aberration in the target language. And that which sounds like an aberration in the target language will not do justice to the original, because a different and contrary impression will be created. If the expression in question is natural to the source language, then surely the translator is obliged to find an expression of equal weight which will transfer the natural sense, thereby abandoning literalness to the source in order to preserve the atmosphere conveyed by the original. And the difficulty is intensified when the source language as a whole is accustomed to using 'higher' language than is normal in the target for describing day to day situations. And so we touch on one of the problems involved in translating from Hebrew to English. The English language is expressed on a different level from that of Hebrew, even in the situations which are common

---

[1] I.e. 'The interlinear version of Holy Scripture is the model or ideal for all translation'. For English version, see in *Illuminations* (New York, 1969).

to both, and if the translator wishes to convey the source language with literal fidelity he will perhaps be guilty of distorting the intention and the implications of the original. And he may, in order to identify the natural context, depart from the equivalent linguistic elements to find the level appropriate to the target language.

* *

There exists a considerable gap between levels on which the English and Hebrew languages are expressed. In the language of daily newspapers in Israel, for example, exaggeration and hyperbole are accepted as normal. In Israel, a man does not simply die, he departs this life. In general, at the time of his departure he is not a man at all. A black-fringed headline will cry out 'The crown of our head has fallen'. If journalists in England were to employ such a style in their newspapers, the results would be most astonishing. Not only would they be guilty of bad taste, but they would be suspected of satirical intentions. And what is the difference? In Israel, such a style of expression is acceptable in this kind of context. In English where the fashion is understatement, the case is different. So in order to convey the original intention the English translator is obliged to find a suitable equivalent by using other words, lowering the tone so as to preserve the spirit of the original. In English we are sorry to announce the death of so-and-so, the crown of our head does not fall. And conversely, in Hebrew, the tone must be raised to produce the parallel result.

It is not surprising that this is also the rule in higher forms of literature. For as the language becomes specialised, and characteristic concepts rooted in Hebrew tradition are expressed, so the difficulty of translation increases. With the emphatic and constant difference in linguistic level a solution is required not only for the translation of individual words or groups of words, but in the overall translation of the work. I shall comment here on early modern Hebrew literature, the quest for an individual style in the literary Hebrew language and the discovery of מליצה *melitzah* (poetic style in prose), the special moulding of the Hebrew language and, at a later stage, the departure from high language to the language of the street, a humbler and simpler language. I shall also discuss a contrary process, towards a variegated and ornate or idiosyncratic style, both in poetry and in fiction. Linguistically, they have to be considered in relation to each other.

The tradition of מליצה *melitzah* is of long standing in Hebrew literature. מליצה *melitzah* comprises fixed linguistic forms interwoven in the widest literary context, drawn from ancient sources. Those are in the main, from the Scriptures, and at times from Rabbinical literature. Old Palestinian Hebrew פיוט *piyut* (lyric poetry) took embellishments from the מדרשים (Rabbinical commentaries on the Scriptures) and the poetry of the Middle Ages relied to a considerable extent on Biblical passages. The *maqama* (a genre of Arabic rhymed prose) behaved similarly. This trend was strengthened during the *Haskalah*, whose spokesmen sought to revive the Scriptural past in the present, sometimes going so far as to use Scriptural language exclusively. Their intention in this was to demonstrate sympathy for and affinity with the Scriptural source and to turn their backs on the developments of the language in the medieval period. Sometimes they created a language of their own in a context of Biblical narrative, as did Abraham Mapu (1808-1868) who in 1853 wrote a novel (his first) entitled אהבת ציין *Ahavath Tzion* "Love of Zion". The language and style of the book are clear imitations of the Scriptures and even the setting of the story is in the land of Judah in the period of the first Isaiah. Mapu was attempting to write according to the spirit of the Bible and to create something outside the limits of his time. He thus created, consciously, an archaic language, with a moral direction such as could only be acceptable in a Scriptural story. All this was 'supposing', for the writer is aware that his readers know that what is written is not a Biblical story, in spite of its disguise. There is no special problem in the transmission of the story or in its translation and transference to another language. The reader will accept this 'supposing'; he knows that he is confronted by archaism and similarly the translator will treat the material as archaic. Such material, which so conspicuously creates a special style, makes the translator's task easier. In every language, the writer has a well-known and much-translated source for imitation, and so the translator does not need to exert himself unduly in his search for a model. He can treat this 19th century material as if it were the Bible itself. For this the tools of translation and the justification for their use are provided by the author. The translator needs only to decide on which style of Biblical translation he wishes to base himself.

The difficulty increases with the application of these tools to another purpose. There were Haskalah writers (including to some extent Mapu himself in עיט צבוע *Ayit tzavu'a* "The coloured falcon") who applied archaic language to stories set in their own time. Now the intention of the writer or of the story (if the intention of the story is discernible) is not so crisply defined. For the writer choosing to write Hebrew, the choice is limited. Since he does not live in a Hebrew environment and knows the language only from literary sources, he has no language of everyday usage to call upon, even if he so desires. In the writing of dialogue there is an additional 'supposing' language; i.e., supposing that these characters were to speak Hebrew (a language of the past), how would they express themselves? And according to his command of the Hebrew language and his knowledge of the relevant literary sources, he devises a solution. Peretz Smolenskin (1842-1885) sought to describe his Jewish environment in a detailed and precise manner. But the tools at his disposal were not much superior to those of Mapu. התועה בדרכי החיים *Hato'eh bedarkhe hahayim* "The wanderer in the paths of life",[2] claims to reflect the lives of contemporary Jews, though there is no denying that the descriptions contain a large measure of tendentiousness. The author seeks to preach and to reform and claims that in his judgement, the state of affairs justifies his acerbity. For this he requires a natural expression, and in the absence of a rich natural language, vibrant and alive, he must stretch to the limits the language inherited from his predecessors. And the results are not satisfactory. Here the first person narrator describes his feelings: 'And even now after twenty years have passed over me since then, with so many changes and reversals: joy and moaning, pleasure and harm, even now I am more stiff-necked than before, only tears shall awake new feelings in my heart and I myself shall not know why'. The language is convoluted, ornate and lacking in sharpness. What is the translator to do? If he treats the whole as if the origin was Biblical he will distort the intention of the story, which is realistic and written with a purpose (according to the limits of the period). He must therefore look beyond the printed word and identify the trend of the story, then convey it with greater economy and with the resources of a living language. Problems like this fell to the lot

---

[2] The fourth and final section was published in 1876.

22

of every writer of the period until the appearance on the scene of Mendeli Mocher Sforim, who, by uncovering additional and hitherto unexploited levels of language, plumbed richer and more dependable sources providing equivalents to what he had previously written in Yiddish. In order to deepen and enrich the language and to widen its scope before its revival as a vernacular, there was a need to liberate it at all levels and to make use of Aramaic as well as a means of adding colour

* * *

In the period of the revival of literary Hebrew, its writers, who had already inherited a tradition of literature with a modernising consciousness, and were thereby also rooted in a deep Hebrew cultural legacy, played on the Hebrew instrument with conspicuous control. Their language was no longer just ornamental but a fundamental expression of Jewishness. It is true that they relied to a great extent on fixed linguistic forms but beside them they used material of elaboration which was not solid and fixed. With Mapu and Smolenskin, Scriptural insertions are simply transferred to another context without any attempt at adaptation. With Bialik and Agnon the position is transformed. In their mature writings, linguistic forms are unobtrusive, because the writers knew how to exploit the linguistic source in order to embrace a new product. In the poem עַל הַשְׁחִיטָה *Al hashehitah* "On the Slaughter", for example, H. N. Bialik blends in a hint at the traditional blessing in turning the reader's attention to slaughter in a ghetto. With the concealed hint at blessing (*Shehita* is *ritual* slaughter) he compares man to the beast, thus (we are invited to think) the point has been reached where human beings too are handed over to the (ritual) slaughterer. He wants to protest but there is no-one to whom he can turn directly and so he requires both a 'way' and a messenger which is 'Heaven'. Even his powers are limited: 'the arm is weary and there is no more hope'. In this poem he also turns the Talmudic verse 'And let justice pierce the mountain' into another form 'And let blood pierce the abyss'. By this is meant that in the meantime a certain measure of straight-forward justice has been lost and so he has no means of moving worlds with his thunder. Justice is in short supply but there is plenty of blood. The poet is thus creating something original and special out of the well-worn material. His linguistic sources have been enriched by additional strata, for, at the

23

beginning of his career, like many of the poets of *Hibath Tziyon*[3] he was basically content with the Biblical stratum. In אל הצפור *El hatzipor* "To the Bird" the images come straight from the Bible: 'Does the rain fall like pearls on Mount Hermon / Does it fall and descend like tears'? As a result of this, the general impression that emerges from the poem is not one of novelty. He has no course but to weep and be silent, says the mourner over the destruction of Zion. 'The tears have ceased, all, all is at an end / but no end has come to my grief'. But when an original, personal and authentic voice is revealed, he enlists the support of new sources and puts them in a creative melting pot. In the poem דבר *Davar* "Word" he is dealing with the experience of Isaiah. The situation recreated is deliberately drawn from Isaiah,[4] the prophet's encounter with God and his call to the prophetic mission. But he alters the prophet's words and transforms the situation. Now it is the poet who addresses the prophet in anger and commands him to flee: 'Cast off from your altar the flare of the fire, O prophet' he says. This means that the time is not yet ripe for prophecy because those who hear it have betrayed it. 'They suffer your pain and they hope your hope—but their souls / aspire to your altar's destruction'. Not only is the language here loaded with holy relics, but it also exploits the accompanying memory as a means of going against the sanctified Scriptural tradition. It is as if the poet draws a dividing line between the past and the present, for now, in our world, there is no-one to hear our cry: 'And great is the chaos around and terrible is the chaos / and there is no escape / and when we cry out in the dark and when we pray—whose ear shall hear'? With this Scriptural language that challenges the fundamental certainty of the Scriptural context, he strengthens and intensifies his plea. This is the motive force of the poem, so the translator must find an echo appropriate to it and not lose the intention of the poem.

With S. Y. Agnon the position is similar, because this writer is deeply rooted in a linguistic tradition heavily laden with associations. But he employs two types of language according to the two Hebrew styles which were created one after the other, and which were later used in combination, Scriptural language and Rabbinical language. In his earlier period of

[3] Lit. 'Love of Zion' — a precursor of the Zionist movement.
[4] See chap. VI.

writing Hebrew, the author was inclined rather to employ Scriptural language (not exclusively) as in the story והיה העקוב למישור *Vehayah he'aqov lemishor* "And the crooked shall be made straight".[5] There he uses forms which has almost disappeared from post-Biblical Hebrew (such as אנכי *anochi* 'I'), suffixes characteristic of the Bible (e.g. *reitim* 'I saw him') the 'waw conversive' ('And-they-shall-fear'—'And they feared'), the word *ki* instead of *she* (for 'that') and a great number of expressions taken from the Bible ('Blessed are they that wait for him') etc., etc. The syntax too recalls the syntax of the Scriptures, as in the opening of the story in these terms: 'Not many years ago there lived in the town of Buczacz, may the Lord bless it, a certain Jew who was upright and honest and his name was Menashe Hayyim Ha-Cohen, a child of the holy community of Yazuvlicz, and although he was not among the mighty of the land and his place was not among the prices of the people, his living was profitable and not frugal in a grocery shop and he lived with his wife Mrs Karindil Charni, for the Lord was kind to him from his youth and he ate bread in plenty, he and his wife with him and he did justice and kindness all his life ...'. The language is not exclusively Biblical; there are later elements. But, the prevailing atmosphere is Biblical, as in the title of the work itself. In saying 'the crooked shall be made straight' in the Scriptural source, the Prophet is commenting on the might of God and his unassailable control. Agnon, on the contrary, is seeking a solution to the contradictions in life and points in a general moral direction, at the compensation for the evil in life, in actions bound up in death.

The second phase in Agnon's language came to expression in a novel such as הכנסת כלה *Hakhnasath kalah* "Bringing in the bride" which was written in the twenties and first published in 1931. Here, as suits his theme, the writer adopts a clearly Rabbinical style to tell his story which turns upon the duty hinted at in the title. We see the development of his language in the use of forms like לישב *leshev* for לשבת *lasheveth* ('to sit'), in the abandoning of the 'waw conversive', in a habit so characteristic of Agnon the storyteller—that of concealing dialogue in a continuous description. The language is full of importations from Rabbinical literature: 'Reb Zechariah son-in-law of Reb Ephraim said, is this all that we have against Reb Israel

[5] Written in 1912.

Shlomo?' The source for this is found in the Mishna,[6] in the argument between the Sadducees and the Pharisees concerning the sanctity of the Holy Writings. 'The Sadducees say, we complain against you Pharisees that you say that the Holy Scriptures defile the hands and the writings of Homer do not defile the hands. Reb Yochanan Ben Zachai said, is this all that we have against the Pharisees?' In this passage, the Pharisees defend themselves against attack from the Sadducees and insist that 'the degree of defilement depends on the degree of our love'. Yochanan Ben Zachai's saying is ironic. It is as if he means that the Pharisees are guilty of more than this, and from there he goes on to argue that they are in fact defending the Torah. In Agnon's version there is a concealed hint at the accusation and the defence, and thus by implication he defends Reb Israel Shlomo. Every language has its realm of associations. If the reader ignores these disguised intentions he will strike the target of the writer who clothes his words in this secretive guise. Intricate associations from the most ancient writings of the Jews must be fully understood and conveyed. This is the real difficulty. Here is an obstacle in the path of the translator who is not capable of taking over such subtleties and expressing them in the target language.

* * *

But there is another type of problem in communication. In the words of some Hebrew writers, the entire direction and tone of voice can be quite different from what is normal, for example, in English literature. Frequently the Hebrew writer, both in the period of Haskalah and in the period of Revival, attempts to give his reader a moral lesson. He is not content solely with providing entertainment, and even a poet like Saul Tchernichovsky, so remarkable for his admiration of beauty and his pure aestheticism, seeks to deliver a sermon. In the English tradition this didactic theme is not so much in evidence because of the tendency of English poetry to amplify the personal voice and to minimise the theme of social argument. If we seek a parallel to the Hebrew tone, we must go back to the generation of Pope, or choose a solitary voice which now sounds archaic, like that of Kipling in his well-known poem 'If'. In English poetry such a tone is rare, whereas in Hebrew poetry the conspicuous direction is didactic and tending towards the

6 Yadayim 4:6.

universal. 'Man is nothing but a tiny scrap of land' thunders Tchernichovsky, going on to define the eternal nature of man, fixed for ever and never changing. In the second stanza, the poet touches on the individual nature of man implanted at the time of his birth. But this follows hard on the heels of his general definition of 'man'. 'Man is nothing but a tiny scrap of land, / nothing but the product of the panorama of his birth, / only what his ear took in while it was still fresh, / only what his eye absorbed before it had its fill of seeing ...'. His poetry sounds like a remonstration, with its reiterations and admonitions, its convuluted sentences, its calls upon earth and heaven. Here and elsewhere the poet identifies the strong feeling of attraction that he has towards the forces of the wild, of the night. This is the drift of Tchernichovsky's poetry; descriptions of the self are blended with startling assertions which throw a light on the progress of the soul and its desires. In discussing the formation of the soul he expresses an ideology too—admiration of beauty, heroism, nature and the people. He sees himself as a 'strange plant' to his people, but at the same time he presents himself as an example of the miraculous. He is wild, he is also free, 'A beast that knows the light of God, that has not borne the yoke'. All the others, who scoff at this message, are 'mummies of flesh and spirit and idolatrous doctors'. At the end of this poem (נטע זר את לעמך 'You are a strange plant to your people') he draws a sharp contrast between them 'For you you are the spring and they are the filth of the pit, / for them the stink of the tomb and for you the joy of light'. In this there is visible a view of himself not only as a poet, as a man bringing entertainment to the people, but also as a preacher, a 'prophet', offering his people a new 'word'. Here he foretells the coming of the 'spring', that is, a symbol of new life, and the 'light', not the light of the Haskalah nor the personal light of Bialik, but his own special light expressed by means of these powerful lines foretelling the coming of a new Messiah who will smite the old a mortal blow. Needless to say, such tidings will not be readily acceptable by a lighter, more sceptical and less ideological spirit.

Such a feeling did not pass away from the world of Hebrew literature with the generation of the writers of the 'Revival'. In our own times, U. Z. Greenberg (1896-1982) who began his literary career during the First World War, in spite of his reservations about the bright prophecies of Tchernichovsky, continued to the end to express in his writings a universal and sermonising line. He too wrote about himself, about the Jew in past times, and, in greater detail, in his own day, about man as man—born of a mother and destined for death: 'Man dies in the valley' he proclaims in the third poem of the collection שירים בשולי שמים *Shirim beshuley shamayim* (Poems on the fringes of Heaven). The series begins with a personal expression and a description of the self to the father and the mother and their relationships to it. He finds himself now '... the only son / sole survivor / in the world', and from this point the compass of the poems seems to broaden, and comes to a universal conclusion concerning the state of man, his birth and his death in the poem אדם מת בגיא *Adam meth bagay* (Man dies in the valley). His birth: 'On the highest of summits: joy, / the man is born', and his death: 'But no man dies on the summit / man leaves the cradle and grows-down-to-the-valley'. Man, according to Greenberg, is born on a pinnacle and ends his days on the plain, and the crucial point is—that during this descent, his isolation is exposed; his mother is not with him: 'and the mother is not then in the valley'. He clothes the familiar statement that 'Man dies alone' in a realistic and picturesque guise—he dies without the consoling shape of the mother that he has already described. Greenberg moves between anger and sadness, between a vibrant national sense and a sense of the isolation of man—all of this bound up with the personality of the self as expressed in poetry. But the central core is a declaration, universal, sometimes strident, very Hebrew and rooted emphatically in the sources. And there is a problem here for the translator. It is generally the opinion of translators that the poetry of U. Z. Greenberg does not lend itself to translation.

* * *

There is another trend in modern Hebrew literature. In poetry—it is the quest for the quiet and simple word, the search for the symbol that travels deep into the individual consciousness. Something similar to the fiction of U. N. Gnessin was created by Abraham Ben-Yitzhak (1883-1950) in his few poems. The hero of his poem is nature with its all-embracing harmony: 'Dreaming lights / pale lights / sink at my feet. / Soft shadows / weary shadows shall caress my path'. (From the poem אלול

28

בשדירה *Elul bisederah* "September in the avenue".[7] He pays homage to quiet with flexible rhymes and Scriptural language. He urges the 'Daughter of the night' 'sit quietly', and in his last poem, written in 1930, on the verge of the prolonged silence leading up to his death, he presents his credo: 'Blessed are they that sow and shall not reap / for they shall wander far', and further on 'Blessed are they that know what their hearts cry out from the desert / and stillness shall blossom on their lips'. And the last stanza: 'Blessed are they for they shall be gathered into the heart of the world / wrapped in the cloak of oblivion / and their eternal law shall be unspoken'. This is the type that he admires, the man who foregoes his happiness to give it to others and lives quietly ('unspoken'). Such a symbolic approach also stamped its mark on later Hebrew poetry. Leah Goldberg (1911-1971) especially, who so admired Ben-Yitzhak, followed in his footsteps even in her later poems which examine death: 'I went into that night /that has no end / and suddenly it was morning / and the sun shone upon the face of the living / who envy the dead', and she ends in a despair that does not complain: 'We were young without hope / we grew up without faith / we grow old without complaints'. And Goldberg was not the only one to compose symbolic poetry. David Vogel (1891-1943) expresses a decisive contrast between light and dark, night and day, to describe his fears. 'In the quiet of the night / the tears of the child are poured out to a distant mother / and he will not be silent. /—for man shall die in the world / behold death is before us'. And at the end of the same poem (from his later period): 'naked thoughts / from yesterday and before await there / to afflict us through the night /—is it not hidden from us'? Or in another poem: 'Through the black nights the convey winds slowly / and where shall it lead us'? on the one hand, and the contrast: 'In the distance shall shine for a moment / a lonely, dull light, / and it shall vanish'. But danger always exists: 'Perhaps a dark riverbed will whisper in my path'. And the end confirms the possibility: 'A dead halting-place / shall gaze after me with longing / through the black night / the convoy sets out'.

In the generation of the State (in Israeli literature) the best known poets sought means of simplifying their language. Y. Amichai (born 1924) strove to come to terms with the new

---

[7] Composed in 1903.

reality in an uncompromising fashion. He conveys to his readers familiar and shared sensations without creating a personal symbolic world of his own. He writes about the war, about loss of faith, and about his relationship with his parents as representing another generation that has also been lost. And all these elements are linked in his writings as components of the contemporary Israeli consciousness expressed in a naturalistic language of the street. Nature is indifferent to the catastrophe of life that surrounds him as he describes the battlefield: 'Rain falls on the faces of my comrades / my living comrades; who / cover their heads with a blanket / and on the faces of my dead comrades, who / no longer cover their heads'. Here, the language of the poet cannot be defined either as Scriptural or Mishnaic, It is colloquial, every-day. The new style is a Sabra style. Clearly the poet knows how to use source material so as to emphasise the sense of loss that pervades his poetry. But this is a conscious technique, an imposition from outside, as when he says 'My parents wove me a destiny of many colours / I grew, and my arm outgrew the sleeve / my destiny did not grow with me'. In his use of the word *pasim*,[8] he is reminding us of Joseph's coat of many colours, and of the fact that he was chosen by his father to accomplish a particular mission. In the terms of the poem, the poet was in a similar position; but now, he puts on the same coat in his adulthood, a coat that does not fit him now, because in the meantime he has grown and developed and has been weaned of what he inherited from his parents. This is a new generation, cut off from what went before. The world is different now; it is empty of mercy, as is written in the poem 'God full of mercy': 'If the world were full of mercy, mercy would be in the world and not only in Him'. From his personal experience, and on the basis of the experience of his entire generation, he denies the existence of mercy, and as a result of this, the influential existence of God. His activity is not perceived in the real world.

Nathan Zach (born 1930) also chooses a natural popular style, although his themes are different. Here is an example of the simplicity of his language: 'I saw a bird of great beauty. / The bird saw me. / A bird of such beauty I shall never see again / to the day that I die. / A ray of sunlight passed over me. / I spoke

[8] There are various translations of the word e.g. 'stripes', 'many colours', 'sleeves'.

words of peace. / The words that I said yesterday / I shall not repeat today'. *Tzipor shniyah* (A second bird) from כל החלב והדבש *Kol hehalav wehadevash* (All the milk and honey). The whole poem is written in a style that is conversational, simple and unadorned, and extremely limited. The experience described is seeing a bird—just a bird. The reader does not know what kind of a bird is in question here. He only knows that to the poet the bird is beautiful, and that the poet declares that the sight is a once-only event. He will never again see such a bird, and he will not speak again as he spoke 'yesterday'. This poem, like many of the poems of Zach, hinges on time, on the past and the present, on the future as well. Man tries to revive the past and is not capable of it, only the memory remains. He writes about exquisite moods, intermediate moods. For example: 'I am not yet ripe for love and I / am still preparing'. And through this, others may prepare themselves for love: 'Lovers may go over / the notes I have made and use them in their lives'. עדיין איני בשל לאהבה *Adayin eyni bashel leahavah* (I am not yet ripe for love). And what concerns him most is the total isolation of man: 'It is not good for man to be alone. / But he is alone nevertheless. / He waits and he is alone and he tarries and he is alone / and he alone knows / that even if he tarries / he shall surely come' (לבדו *Levado* (Alone) from שירים שונים *Shirim shonim* (Different Poems)). The poet builds his theme on the basis of two Biblical passages, from Genesis 2.18, God's declaration that the man needs a wife, and from Habakkuk 2.3, the promise of the Lord that a Redeemer will come. It is man who waits, the Redeemer who tarries. In this poem they are one and the same, and one thing unites them, that they are alone. He takes the statement by God that 'It is not good for man to be alone' and replies 'But he is alone nevertheless'. There is no escape from loneliness.

* * *

In the work of younger writers too there is a tendency towards a different linguistic trend both in fiction and in poetry. The writer A. Appelfeld seeks to create a certain atmosphere and a definite type of inter-personal relationship by means of an idiosyncratic metaphorical style. He attempts to capture the frozen moment and make human relationships stand still and by these means he perpetuates the situation that has passed and that still casts its shadow on the present. He infuses into his words a strange, symbolic element as in this description of winter: 'The winter like a dark flock of birds came down in the night and stayed'.[9] Thus the night takes on the dimension of threat in 'a dark flock of birds'. The image of birds is a prevalent one in Appelfeld's stories, and he lays great stress on the seasons and their changes. Here is another description of winter: 'In the night the winter's end flowed as within a transparent bell'.[10] The image of the bell is also a familiar one in his work. In the startling linking together of night and bell, and in the description of its action as that of flowing (something we do not normally associate with night), the writer forces us to look at things from a different angle. He not only tells us that the night is slow-moving, but also in the rhythm of the writing he stirs a slow echo. The words create the impression described, as in the continuation: 'A man with an umbrella in his hand, a woman in a summer dress, a car parked at the roadside, a scrap of mist clinging to the wall. Nothing, nothing, only the slow pulse'. This leap prepares us for the encounter with the plot which is the revival of the frozen past. For the man, Gruzman, meets again the woman whom he knew from 'somewhere', whence she now appears. Gruzman has spent the interim years in Jerusalem, is on the point of losing contact with that existence: 'And now he felt the years in Jerusalem had stripped him of everything, he was left unconnected'. And now, with the renewal of the link, he is obliged, insofar as it is possible, to make the connections again. Gruzman is not prepared for this, and in his parting from Betty with whom he was linked somewhere in the past, he loses his inner self. In the hospital to which she has been sent, he ponders: 'He had nothing. There was nothing in him but the love in the pity that he felt for these creatues coming and going ... he felt now that without this love he had no existence'. The novel identifies a sort of liberation from ties in the face of death. Of course, the writer knows how to change the rhythm. He demonstrates this in the novella באדנהיים עיר נופש *Badenhaym, ir no'esh* (Badenheim, holiday resort) [11] where the pace is much more lively, the sentences shorter and the plot more extensive.

[9] From the story לחשי הקור *Lahashey hakor* (Whispers of the cold) in אדני הנהר *Adney hanahar* (Pedestals of the river, 1971).

[10] From the novel העור והכתנת *Ha'or wehakuthoneth* (Skin and clothes, 1971).

[11] In the volume *Shanim wesha'oth* (Hours and years, 1975).

A special metaphorical style of a different kind is seen in the work of the authoress A. Kahana-Carmon. In her stories even the language of dialogue is colourful, ornate and literary, and there is none of the casual language of the street employed by most Israeli fiction in imitation of reality. This comes about through brief snatches of conversation: 'We frequently visit your gardens' (קבועות *qvu'oth* 'regular' used adverbially instead of הרבה *harbeh* 'much'). 'We have never met a man' (איש *ish* 'man' instead of מישהו *mishehu* 'anyone') from the story החמה נסתלקה *Ha hamah nistalqah* ('The sun went).[12] The storyteller takes the reader still further from everyday reality by the use of startling archaism, with the use of the waw conversive for example: 'He opened his mouth and-will-speak (= and spoke)' she says of 'the man who lived on a star' the student to whom the teacher (the first person narrator) is attracted in אח וא מצאתי חן *Im na matzati hen* (If I have found favour). By linguistic means the writer succeeds in imposing upon her descriptions a higher level, giving an added dimension to the factual material. For what distinguishes and sets apart her work is the particular view of the narrator in the story, an intensive view that enlarges and redoubles every detail and imposes on the plot an unusual perspective. Even the titles of the stories bear this out: 'If I have found favour' or לב הקיץ לב האור *Lev haqayitz, lev haor*, (Heart of the summer, heart of light'. Her theory of art is expressed perhaps in the words of the writer to the puppet in מושכלות ראשונים *Muskaloth rishonim* (Axioms): 'All that is in my power is to approach the simplicity of things by means of a personal, original relationship. Sifting the particular detail that stresses the phenomenon as it is, I must give it clear expression, born of reality, striking with a mild concussion; either vibrant surprise or a ray of light piercing to know once and for all without pronouncing judgement. Or like a widening in perception, in sympathy'. In other words, the writer chooses a minor detail, sifts it, takes hold of it, intensifies it, all through the medium of a particular linguistic mode.

* * *

And in the work of the younger Hebrew poets a romantic trend has been revived. Elsewhere I have described this

---

[12] From the collection *Bikhfifah ahath* (Under one roof, 1966).

phenomenon in greater detail.[13] I will comment here only on the work of the poetess Yonah Wallach, who evokes other-worldly, distant, drugged sensations. Most of her poems are constructed as one long and involved sentence. They are full of dreams; world like כיסופים *kisufim* (yearning) and כמיהה *kemihah* (pining) play a central role in them. The syntax is complicated: 'When Frederic imitated the walking of / Niztah he fainted from yearning', (in the poem *Niztah*)[14] or: 'What is your name Christina / Christina thinks and tries to feel / the circle closes tight round Christina / the pining makes her weak' (from the poem 'Christina'). Sometimes she tries to defend herself against the real truth and against the secret: 'With a Swedish key Lotta combs her hair / her hairs are steel springs / she takes pills against thevarious feelings of mystery'. And she (Lotta that is) is blind now to the completeness of the matter: 'What / Lotta takes in place / of the truth is that you have a wonderful body'. And the result is that she is no longer responsive to symbols ('the incense of war'): 'And now she understands only words' (from the poem 'Lotta'). Her poetry always points to another place, to somewhere and also beyond it. In another poem she tries to identify the two points; 'There' and 'Beyond'. 'There there are storms there there is lightning / there there are voices and stone upon trees / there shining silver and there there is life / and on the other side they are silent and hidden'. (In the poem שם יש *sham yesh* (There there is). The contrast of motion and stillness is sharply drawn, and the poem ends: 'There they play on pipes to standing corpses / and on the other side they are hidden and do not flow'. Her poetry expresses a kind of revival of prophetic eschatological vision, but here the vision is personal and private; the disembodiment of the physical, the departure from self: 'Let them come and bring me food / I may die but let them come / let them bring me sweets / let them enter and wrap me in wrappings / and put something warm on my tooth / and say to me all kinds of things / let them enter and bring me things / let them stand around / and I shall be well and sweetwarm / let them stand / and I my own self forgetting / let them stand here and I forgetting myself / and yes, let them come and be like two children' (in the poem שהם יבואו *Shehem*

[13] Leon I. Yudkin: *Escape into siege* (London. Boston, 1974) chap. 11 especially pp. 159-164.

[14] All quotations are from *Shirah* (Tel Aviv, 1976).

yavou (Let them come). She seeks an experience that is beyond this world and beyond death too. She strives to expand the bounds of personal experience and to restore to life the symbol of light: 'To the other side I cross like a bridge / the Messiah a little boy passes beneath me / suddenly there is light and living children'. (From the poem) כלה- *kol ha-* (All the ...).

The best known recent Israeli fiction has turned in a similar direction. From local material the two writers A. B. Yehoshua (born 1937) and A. Oz (born 1939) create suprarealistic situations. Yehoshua tends in his later stories and particularly in his novel המאהב *Hameahev* (The lover, 1978) to cut out a slice from the Israeli scene, to people it with familiar types and to construct the plot on historical events, and to open the story in a most unexpected direction. Examination of every story will prove that this is so, and will expose murky depths in the hearts of the protagonist—hatred of the father towards his son, hatred of the lover towards the son of the woman he loves, hatred of the Israeli towards his homeland. A world of savagery and conflict is spread out beneath the calm and orderly surface. In most of his stories there is a startling development or even a circular plot which leaves the beginning and the end open, like בתחלת קיץ *1970* *Bitehilath qayitz 1970* (Beginning of summer 1970, 1972). One of the Yehoshua's favourite words is *nidham* (astonished)—the characters in his stories are frequently astonished, even at hearing something familiar: 'And again he was astonished to hear the low price' (from the story יום שרב ארוך *Yom sharav arokh* (A long day's heat) at hearing the low price offered for the broken-down car of the ageing mechanic. The writer's language is dry and factual, like the protocol of a meeting. The sentences are short and so the conspicuous words are the more noisy and startling. At the beginning of the story שלשה ימים וילד *Shloshah yamim wayeled* (Three days and a child),[15] which is written in the first person, the author sets out the course of events as they happened in that far distant time: 'I had thought that I would have to apologise: but it is as if things have been reversed. The three-year old son of a woman I love was entrusted to my care in the last days of the holiday, in the first days of the autumn in Jerusalem. At first I thought about the child, then I wanted to kill him. But it was not within my power. I must still try to discover what prevented me. In any

---

[15] In מול היערות *Mul hayearoth* (Opposite the Forests, 1965).

case, the time and the place were right'. The reader must come to terms with a murderous intention for which he is unprepared. On the contrary from what he has learnt so far, the reader may expect a sense of warmth on the part of the lover towards the son of the woman he loves. Such at least is generally to be expected of a man in love. All the difficulties and dangers that beset the child in the course of these days confirm this fundamental awareness. Perhaps, in the life of man these feelings do exist, whether he does not admit them or is unconscious of them. In Yehoshua's stories the subconscious floats up to the surface, and the personality speaking through the story expresses it. Or, otherwise, the story itself puts on a skin that leaves no room for doubt. Secret fears are revealed in the sharp reversals in the stories. In the story שתיקה הולכת ונמשכת של משורר *Shetiqah holekheth wenimshekheth shel meshorer* (Continuing silence of the poet) in the same volume, the father (the silent poet) and the mentally handicapped son exchange roles. The son starts composing poetry and signing it with his father's name. The poetry which the father sees he describes as 'mad, unbalanced, complicated, lines cut short for no reason, startling rhymes, erratic pointing'. Here the father is not aware of the terror that he strives to control. The fact speaks for him. The poet who has grown old passes away, and a new essence, according to what is recounted here, enters and penetrates him.

Fear and menace fill the world of Amos Oz. In the novel מקום אחר *Maqom aher* (Another place, 1966) from its beginning with the detailed description of kibbutz Metzudath Ram, the writer hints at a dimension additional to what exists, and this is the other place. Apparently 'Our village was built in an optimistic spirit', and in fact, the underlying forces that ferment beneath it are always threatening and laying a stranglehold on its source of life. The struggle between Reuven the kibbutznik and Siegfried the visitor expresses this. 'Dark creatures emerged from their lairs and came out to injure and destroy.' Siegfried is the business partner of the man who stole Reuven's wife. Now he himself is about to take his daughter from him. The expectation of destruction is always present, and even Reuven the responsible and good-natured expresses it. In conflict with Berger he dies for reasons which are not clear. And the conclusion drawn from the action of these strange forces leads to a clear focus in the last paragraph of the book. 'On the distant chair falls a circle of light. No man sits there. Do not see these men and women who belong to another place. You must listen to the rain lashing the windows. Look only at the people enclosed here, in the warm room. Move aside every obscuring screen'. And then (in the last sentence) you may 'call this picture by the name of love'. The encounter with danger moves between fear (or nausea) and fascination. Sometimes the stories of Oz operate on both levels at once, or at times in reality, at times in fantasy, as in מיכאל שלי *Mikhael sheli* (My Michael, 1966). When the heroine (Hannah the narrator) expresses her longings as bound up in the form of the two Arab twins whom she has known since her youth (and who play such an active role in her imagination) at the end of the novel, she surrenders herself entirely to the vision of destruction: 'But not only words are left to me. It is still in my power to shift a heavy lock. To swing open iron doors, to set free the two twin brothers. They shall slip quietly over the plain by night, I shall incite them'. The twins here are Hannah's agents of violence, her representatives in fulfilling the destined and sought for role. And all this destruction speaks 'a caress full of desire' that ends in 'cold tranquillity'. The confusion of fear and desire is expressed to an extreme degree in the story נוודים וצפע *Nawadim wa tzefa* (The nomads and the viper),[16] in the encounter between the girl Geulah and the Arab (the nomad). She declares that 'this man was endowed with a repellent beauty' (that is, he possesses two contrary qualities, one attracting and the other repelling). The presence of the jackals testifies to the danger. Does the Bedouin rape her? She goes out once more 'among the bushes' and stretches out on the grass. The snake bites her, but 'the pain is dull, almost a delight'. Her encounter with the Arab who attacks her is like her encounter with the snake; it has a double sense.

In this survey I do not pretend to have touched all the strata of the Hebrew literary language in the twentieth century. For all that, I have hinted at different literary fashions and their modes of expression, and the most important levels that the reader should recognise. Here are five: 1) *Melitzah*—a language taken from the sources and incorporated into the inherited material. 2) The period of revival—an involved language, sometimes

---

[16] In the volume ארצות התן *Artzoth hatan* (Lands of the jackal, 1965).

prophetic and constantly developing. It does not simply become absorbed in the inherited material but itself revives the material and creates something new. 3) Simplicity in language—especially, through the influence of the spoken and changing language, and a turning away from the rhetorical Hebrew of the previous generation. 4) Ornamentation of language and romantic revival. The complexity of the young tradition. 5) The language of extreme personal situations, as revealed in the dry approach of A. B. Yehoshua or in the more convoluted syntax of A. Oz. All these trends are branches integrally linked to the ancient Hebrew stem. The language has changed ideologically and sociolinguistically. It also moves in accordance with the thematic context. Poetry is vastly different from prose at their extreme positions. But prose has to use the language of poetry and, at the least, assume its existence in the background. In general, language aspires to be appropriate to its subject and to its objective.

3

THE SABRA HERO:
      MOSHE SHAMIR'S EARLY NOVELS

The term 'Sabra literature' has been adopted to categorise the
Hebrew literature that began to emerge with the incubation of
Israeli statehood. This literature was produced in the main by
those born within the yishuv who came to literary consciousness at about the time of the War of Independence. Because
these writers were often members of the ginger group of the
Haganah known as the Palmach, their writing is known
alternatively as 'Palmach literature'. It is thus a literature of one
language, time and place, also one of function. These writers
shared a group experience, a social purpose and, with whatever
subsidiary issues that divided them, an ideology. They had
fought to establish a State of the Jews in the Middle East, had
grown up against the background of increasing Arab and
British hostility to the nascent Nation, had witnessed a revival
(even if on a small scale) of Hebrew literature written in the
language now spoken by the group, and wanted to achieve a
position of normality for what was to be a new Nation within
the international community. Their writing constitutes a direct
reflection of this context, commenting on the immediate
external reality in prose and in verse, in lament and in
exaltation, in analytical argument and in declamatory programme.

What is new in the literature? Not the texture of the
language. Hebrew had been used as a literary instrument since
early Biblical times, and the literary language of the Sabras did
not often depart significantly from the accepted stock of
European/Palestinian literary Hebrew of the post-Mendeli
period. Neither was this literature particularly innovatory in
technique. In both prose and verse, greater innovations had
been introduced into Hebrew literature by the prose writers
of the second aliyah such as Y. H. Brenner or such as
U. N. Gnessin (1879-1913) who remained in Europe, and by
the poets of the third aliyah such as U. Z. Greenberg and
A. Shlonsky (1900-1973). So, traditional in their language and
in their literary techniques, they contributed a new dimension to
Hebrew literature in terms of the scope of their concerns and

their subject matter. These were shaped by the circumstances of their early steps. And it is the Hebrew literature of this background that becomes self-consciously Israeli, a new phenomenon, specifically local and native, in fact, Sabra.

In fiction, no one expresses the range of those concerns more than the writer Moshe Shamir (born 1921) in his early novels. He was not only a fiction writer of the new Sabra mould, but also an ideologue of the infant society. I will discuss here only his early work, i.e. those novels which most clearly bear the work of these concerns, and remain within the confines of the immediate Sabra world. Beyond these three novels, הוא הלך בשדות *Hu Halakh Basadoth* (He Walked in the Fields, 1947), תחת השמש *Thahath Hashamesh* (Beneath the Sun, 1950) and במו ידיו *Bemo Yadaw* (With His Own Hands, 1951), he has tried to extend this range in subject matter and technique. But that takes us, in terms of the very rapid movement of Israeli history, beyond my present subject. These novels, as the author himself characterised them (in an editorial comment in the short-lived journal ילקוט הרעים *Yalqut hare'im*) aspire to be not revolutionary in themselves, but adequate to the revolutionary situation that is their subject. The world described is uncrystallised, and so the literature is aware of its freshness. The writer is neither divorced from the situation, nor undetached from it; he is part of it, and so its presenter and commentator.

* * *

As one would expect in such conditions, great stress is placed on the idea and fact of youth. Young people do not so often carry the burden of that other time, other place—the rejected diaspora, in whose context the Jew was rejected too, a foreign society of earlier times. Youth is the symbol of the tabula rasa. Everything can begin now with the Sabra initiating a new Israel. It is no coincidence then that the most striking hero of those novels is the young man, born on the soil of the land, who represents all the potentiality of the future State. An investigation of the qualities of the Shamir hero youth discloses too the ideals of the writer and of the group represented by the writer. הוא הלך בשדות *Hu Halakh Basadoth* centres largely on the fortunes and misfortunes of Uri Cahana who was an 'attractive creature ... with a curl, a bedouin headcover, a knapsack, thinking of a million things at once'. He is strong, able-bodied, sufficiently but not over-reflective, relating totally to the developing situation in such matters as agriculture, security and his own growing manhood. And, above all, he is loyal. However much he is distracted by his own individual impulses and needs, he recognises his social responsibility; 'Why should you, banal promoters of general truths, complain about the nuisance of the public. Like every shilling in the world, there is also another side. And that other side is called the collective sense of responsibility, comradeship, yes, even just comradeship'. What was to be the ideological mouthpiece of the young writers used the same word—comrade (*rea*) to describe itself— ילקוט הרעים *Yalquth hare'im* (Comrades' Anthology). The literature is pervaded by the sense of new common purpose that had to be generated to allow the new society to emerge. Progressive literature provided a focus and an echo, and its chief hero in the novel was the bearer of the message. This rhapsody on Uri is characteristic of the Palmach view of the young world.

Of course, there are older people in the novel too. There are the founders of the kibbutz who rejected the other life. Such as Willy, Uri's father; 'He grasped kibbutz life healthily and totally. Because he knew instinctively that his life was on the kibbutz and nowhere else'. Willy creates the conscious ideology that Uri is to epitomise in his own life. Willy appreciates that in the degree of sacrifice required in this life-style he has abandoned an alternative; 'Out of a feeling that it is the natural life needed, demanding first and foremost, not just a temporary sacrifice, but patient obstinacy for generations'. But in the very fact of his selection of options, Willy is perhaps impaired. The ideal figure has no options. He grows into a particular framework, as a plant in its own soil. He is not too reflective on his own situation because he takes it for granted. And this we can see in the figure of Uri: 'Uri was not enamoured of thinking for its own sake. He would take it up for a moment when something would trouble him or was so significant that it allowed him no rest; but thinking out of the habit of the power of thought in itself, original and independent life of feeling, reaction and analysis, these were symptoms of an unfortunate sickness'. So the intellectual and spiritual functions are a means rather than an end for Uri, whose starting point is the physical environment in whose creation he has to participate. He does have a spiritual dimension but that comes up in the context of the pragmatic, not in the theoretical or the ideological.

Shamir is writing not merely words but a description of

actuality, an actuality where untimely death was always present. The Sabra plant could not grow naturally in the fact of the hostile environment. Shamir wanted to convey his own experiences and his own tragic losses. במו ידיו Bemo Yadaw is written as a tribute to his fallen brother. The Shamir here always bears the sense of a necessary death. So he can only be young; he will never know maturity. Uri fantasises about his own death, which will serve as compensation for all that he has received from his parents. He will be the sacrifice; 'To drop Uri from the picture, to die before them. To cast on them the whole weight of pain destined for our family. To be more exalted and holier than both of them, to suffer more, to be a sacrifice, to give them back everything at once, to lie down, to laugh, and to see how they treasure and cherish all that smacks of the touch of your head or your life'. In במו ידיו Bemo Yadaw too, Elik hugs the presentiment of his own death. This is not a surprising fact, in view of the dangers which he actively courts as a commander in the Palmach. At the celebration of the UN vote of 29 November 1947, favouring the creation of Jewish State, he asks himself who will pay the price. And the answer comes; 'we will pay'. Early death is a datum inseparable from the life style adopted, in fact of the life style into which he he has grown unquestioningly. Such a hero must be always young.

What then is the Sabra? There is an explicit portrait of such a type in the characterisation of the young man in תחת השמש Tahath Hashamesh; 'Aharon was at home. They gave him the appendage 'Sabra', a name which held both blame and affection together. He was in any case a friend of the trees, the shepherd lads, the groove of the wadi, the railway bridges especially if there was water underneath'. We see here how the author singles out Aharon's attachment to the physical environment as his quintessential characteristic. This environment is not merely an external landscape, it is part of his very essence. He says of himself that he must belong in toto; I cannot stand at the side. I must be in everything. I have to be the first, the patron, the overall originator, to be master, to be one, that I myself should exist alone in the world, I myself exist alone. Orchards? Nonsense, these are my very limbs'. The orchards are Israel, and Israel is Aharon who in turn is Israel and the total environment.

* * *

As a result of the consciousness of being new, certain side effects come into view. I have briefly noted that, in terms both of language and literary technique, few radical departures were effected by Shamir. He writes standard literary Hebrew, certainly a crystallised literary vehicle by the 40s. It is true that the dialogue reflects actual speech patterns of the vernacular rather than a theoretical 'as if' language (unspoken), and that description and reflective passages are also peppered with idiomatic interventions and slang. But this does not mark the prose out significantly from non-Sabra prose. And the literary techniques adopted do not reflect the literary experimentation of the late nineteenth and early twentieth centuries. On the contrary, the social realism of the Shamir novel consists of straight description, reflection, flashback, representative dialogues and the traditional use of time and narrator. However, the consciousness of the new in terms of the object described still creates a discontinuity from the past. The Land, its institutions, its people, and particularly its heroes, are not connected with what has gone before. So we have a strange combination of a very traditional literary manner in the service of a soi-disant revolutionary situation. This is quite unlike the literary ambition of the 20s when such as Shlonsky and Greenberg proclaimed the need for new literary forms to match that particular realignment of values and change. In vocabulary, metre and tone, Hebrew poetry consciously reshaped itself, trying to break free from the existing models of Bialik and Tschernichovsky. But now Shamir, in his prose, was not even taking cognisance of earlier experiental Hebrew novelists such as Gnessin, Brenner, Agnon and Vogel. On the contrary, his aspiration was to tell a straight story straight and to shape the narrative according to the values of the dramatis personae.

That the hero lacks roots in what has passed before we can gather not only fro the narraive context, but from specific verbal hints. במו ידיו *Bemo Yadaw* opens with an account of Elik's childhood, a remark that, although jocular, contains a serious grain: 'Elik was born from the sea'. This is a mythical opening that reflects both on the closeness of Elik to his natural surroundings, and on the mysteries of his origins. He has come from the sea, i.e. has not been born into a normal family in the normal way, marking a continuity of generations. This is the new man, the new Jew, the new Israeli; 'And so Elik was born from the sea, which is of course a joke—still, no-one else

43

amongst us was as close to the sea as Elik, as there was no-one else amongst us who would be as close as him to dogs, to horses, to other children, to goats, to trees, to new buildings going up, to excavations in the sand, to machines'. Elik is the person whose natural, unquestioned habitat is contemporary Palestine/Israel, whose geographical and historical situation is unproblematic. Elik's brother who 'tells' the story sees in Elik a sort of emblem of the Sabra, embodying the characteristics outlined above.

In תחת\ השמש, *Tahath Hashamesh*, we have a portrait of a more selfconscious assumption of this total identification. This is how Aharon sees himself in relation to the Land and to his girl friend Balfouria. He would like to know her as well as he knows the Land. The latter, although only reinhabited by the Jews en masse, is not new to him. He tries to locate a historical root for his sense of identification; 'I do not know you yet, Balfouria. I want to know you as well as I know so many, many things. I know this piece of land is mine. I know it better than any unwashed Arab born with his ancestors here hundreds of years ago, because I was born here with my ancestors three thousand years ago. Men like me don't ask many questions. The world belongs to men like me in an absolute sense. They take, and that's that'. The aspiration and the actuality seem to mingle here. Aharon sees himself as a link in Jewish history that is now finding its more natural place back home, and that is too how he feels in the present. Or, at least, that is what he says. The Jew has come back home. And this too is how Balfouria now describes herself. She has borrowed Aharon's own colours which are now her own; 'Here leans a lad whose head is struck in the darkness like a root. Here you are stuck like a root. Nearby, amongst the trees, gleam warm Hebrew lights which we will have perhaps to defend, which we might have to mourn'. The passionate declaration of faith is a covenant of total loyalty to the primary historical root, now the only living actuality.

* * *

The ideological promotion of the closeness to the physical environment may be the result of a revulsion from what was considered as the overspiritualisation of Jewish life. The Zionist idea was not only concern with the reconstitution of the Jewish people in its ancient homeland, but also with a reorientation towards more 'normal' economic pyramid, and towards a more earthbound base. If the nation had to be rebuilt in Palestine it could not be done solely by Middle and East European middlemen, clerics and intellectuals. The land had to be repossessed and sown; it also had to be defended. A new class is called for, a class of primary producers, of workers, of farmers, of soldiers. Traditional Jewish values are a luxury within such a dire context. Even the titles of the early works of Sabra fiction capture this realisation. S. Yizhar's first story is entitled אפרים חוזר לאספסת 'Ephraim returns to the lucerne' (1938), which was followed later by Tammuz's first collection of stories called חולות הזהב *Holoth Hazahav* (Golden Sands, 1950), which relate the impressions of childhood in the emergent State. The three Shamir novels discussed here all bear in their titles this concern with physicality. Things are done with one's own hands, in the bosom of nature, 'beneath the sun'. And that is where he, the hero, walks in the fields. Y. Mosinzon's celebrated play written during the War of Idependence itself, was called בערבות הנגב *Be'arvoth Hanegev* (On the Steppes of the Desert, 1949). These are not the sorts of titles that would have been selected by earlier generations of Hebrew novelists, and neither do the works themselves share such concerns. Mendeli built up a critique of stetl Jewish life. Berdyezewski, Feierberg and Bershadsky treated of the marginal, European Jew, searching for a specific place in the new world. Gnessin's Jew was almost totally European. Brenner's was not, but he was so smitten by the implications of his disastrous, national plight that he could not rehabilitate himself. Neither is the immigrant Hebrew fiction of Agnon, Hazaz, Burla and Shenhar so totally committed to this new Israeli physicality. It all belongs, at least partially and spiritually, to the old world.

Such a description as opens תחת השמש *Tahath Hashamesh* would not naturally have found a place in this European Hebrew literature (it is not necessarily an earlier literature, because there is no natural chronological divide between the two strata in our typology); 'Until the lentils, called fruit, sink to the ground, and again you, the child, are sunk in the tender, cool sand, inspecting the signs of birds' feet therein, with their droppings hardened and gone grey, available for play on the part of ants, who have a very large nest beyond the fence, and can serve as their train, all of them in one long line ...' The

author, through the child's narrative voice, tries to capture the
details of the physical environment, which is so new and
captivating to the infant. The notification is not only an object
in itself, but also a sign of possession. The child rejoices in the
observed and possessed intricacy of pattern.

Presentiment of death (noted above) and intimacy with the
natural world come together in the reflections of the young
hero, at the end of תחת השמש *Tahath Hashamesh*; 'Blood, sand
and sun fall on each other, change each other and change the
world. He drew out thoughtful steps and did not know that
blood, sand, and sun were to accompany him throughout his
life up to the moment when his quick blood would be absorbed
into the soft sand beneath a hard sun'. The climax of the book
serves as a commentary on the title. What happens beneath the
sun is labour, struggle and death. Just as his life is always lived
in the company of the trinity of blood, sand and sun, so is his
death to take place there. All is physical.

The title of במו ידיו *Bemo Yadaw* is also reflected in the
descriptions of the novel. Whatever Elik wants to do, he does
with his own hands. His world is physical, immediately
perceived and held: 'You should know that more than anything, Elik liked eating what his hands made'. And in praise of
anglers: 'Here is the life of a family of fishermen, here is how
they live inside the very things themselves, very near to the
foundations themselves, to the sea, to the fish, to the sand, to
the wind'. He loved working too, and he loved the actual feel of
things: 'Sand hills—listen and feel with your fingertips this
golden tenderness, than which there is nothing purer in the
world ... this pleasure which you enjoy in what is called earth'.
There is an ecstasy in contact. The world is the earth, in the
literal and metaphorical senses of the word.

I can now summarise the ambitions of the Shamir novel, and,
to a considerable degree, that of the beginnings of Sabra fiction.
The author attempted to capture the local reality and to recreate
it in the word. This reality consisted of a small community
striving to establish itself in an inhospitable atmosphere and in
difficult conditions. The non-Jewish population of the area is
becoming increasingly hostile, and the mandatory power, soon
to disappear from the scene, is unhelpful, in the eyes of the
Jewish patriot. But there can also apply negative definitions,

For all the assumptions of Jewish patriotism and the single-minded vision of the necessary struggle, there is no attempt made, certainly not explicitly, at a ratiocination of the ideology. This is done neither by the narrator in the stories nor by the characters described. They live their lives in this way as though there is no choice, and so no selection of options. Action is taken, not as though a decision had been reached through the elimination of alternatives, but as though these alternatives had never been considered in the first place. The less that the character is in a position to consider an alternative, the closer he approaches the assumed ideal. It could be for this reason that the youth in the Shamir novel born in the Land, is, by implication, the more perfect type. Such a person has never known another position, so he is not swayed from his objective. He does not have to justify his stance; it is the only one possible. And unlike people who have emerged from another context, he has no memory of this other. He is in this sense born of the sea. In הוא הלך בשדות *Hu Halakh Basadoth*, Uri is a much simpler character than his young immigrant girlfriend Mika, but, unlike her with her sophisticated European struggles, he is at one with himself, with his life, his work, his country, and his overall objectives.

These novels, although historically situated, are not placed in the context of the past. The Jewish issue is obviously implicit but scarcely mentioned. There is no expressed consciousness of an international and eternal Jewish people, only of a particular group living in the Middle East. Individuals, such as Mika, come from the outside; but they are odd, disjointed. The implied lesson, is that Zionism has come along precisely to repair the breach. The type of the past is Mika, the type of the future is Uri. No more split loyalties or traumas produced by the non-Jewish environment. Now the Jew is responsible for his own fate. And yet the case is not argued by the protagonists. So there is no expressed ideology, although the point comes home clearly enough. The situation is seen from within, not from a detached or objective, critical stance. Shamir's novels, for all the significance of their content, are not works of history or ideology, nor are they expression of Jewish values. None of these things would be strange in the context of such novels. They are, after all, expressly works of social realism.

Their starting point, like their conclusion, is the present. Their ambition is to relate the contemporary history of Israel, and to portray a type, the Sabra, as well as to lament his necessary but cruel fate. במו ידיו *Bemo Yadaw* is a portrait of Elik. But Elik is not just a lone individual, nor even just a member of the group, though he is very much both of these. He is also the reflector of the general mood. At the critical historical moment of the United Nations vote, Elik is the Nation: 'This evening they had promised, after various postponements, the final decision, and now he was convinced that the ferment was pumping its bubbles into his blood. Not into the shops and not into the streets with the traffic, but into his blood'. Elik, then, bears, in his own eyes and perhaps in those of the narrator, the burden of a whole people. Or at least of that particular section of the people, a tribe maybe, which finds itself located in Palestine at this juncture, through its acceptance of a particular task. Maybe, as is then pointed out, everyone else in the great public, open gathering, feels likewise. But that does not invalidate Elik's representative function. After the announce-ment of the UN vote, 'each one felt and well knew that he was celebrating his own personal holiday, and that the whole rejoicing was his own ... thus felt Elik'. There is a complex of related entities here—Elik, his family, the Palmach, the yishuv, and the emergent State. The writer, through a presumed narrator, tries to set these out in a clear and acceptable form, adequate to the circumstances.

War, the struggle, the act of killing, is part of the recognised reality of the Sabra situation. Anyone living in Israel in the post World War period through the 1950s must be aware of war as the primary political issue. But for the ideological Palmach writer, war must be more than an incidental fact. It is a dreadful reality brought about in the specific instance by the possibility of action or the situation of the Sabra. In Shamir's early novels, the fact of war is all-pervasive. These young heroes are imbued with the consciousness that they must fight, that they have to try to kill, and that they are likely to die prematurely. The necessity of this dreadful reality is not often questioned, although Elik does reflect on the matter at one point in במו ידיו *Bemo Yadaw*. He is peacefully asleep for the last time and he would like to remain in this state; 'Why, for goddness's sake is there the sort of world which does not allow you to turn over in your blanket and sleep as much as your sick body desires? You

48

are expected to be very angry, to hate a great deal'. But this is a passing phase. Elik would never succumb to the temptation and renege on his recognised duty. This is his world, his only world. His place is here in the battle, a function contrasted with that of his parents: 'A real world, Elik's day, his activity, his running through fire and on roads—it is a world of mutual pretence'. Elik does not tell his parents of the dangers courted, though these can surely be guessed. The private world of Elik, we are left to assume, has dimensions beyond his own limitations. This is the real world, certainly the real world of the new Sabra cast.

In each of these three early novels, the end, a necessary but individually tragic one, is previously prefigured. In הוא הלך בשדות *Hu Halakh Basadoth*, the story of Uri is related as a flashback by his father Willy. The disaster is announced at the outset and then retailed. תחת השמש *Tahath Hashamesh* (a much more diffuse work) contains the reflection, by the omniscient narrator quoted above, Aharon, who is fated to perish, again prematurely, beneath the sun. So the title of the novel is an expression of that presentiment. And במו ידיו *Bemo Yadaw* announces its own purpose from the outset. It is 'chapters of Elik', a dirge, a tribute and a tale of struggle and death. So it is a sort of holy account, a hagiography devoted to a brother, a Palmach hero and fighter in the common national struggle. All these heroes almost all the time, certainly when it comes to the crunch and action is called for, accept the necessity of this situation even at its most cruel. If they must die, then so be it. 'The queue is getting shorter', as the Palmach saying has it. There is a sense of inescapable rightness in the struggle. Elik reflects early in the novel; 'Now it is war. We saw this today. We must go and conscript. We have to fight them ourselves, that is that. We won't leave the war to others ... We, with our own hands, have to kill Germans, to kill and again to kill and not to stop killing them'. (This is, of course, during the Second World War). The motto of the novels comes over again. Everything must be done 'with one's own hands', even the nastiest (or perhaps, especially the nastiest) of tasks. If killing be necessary for the national struggle, then we are the ones who must carry it out. We cannot in all conscience expect the means necessary to achieve our own purposes to be adopted by others. After all, he might have added, had he articulated the thinking behind his aggressive statement, such would be at odds with the whole exercise, whose aim is to achieve independence of action for the Jewish people. One has to do things for oneself—that is the meaning of freedom.

But this is not worship of war, nor appreciation of war for its own sake. Such an ideological evaluation of war is drawn in תחת השמש *Tahath Hashamesh*, in the feeling of the Revisionist Shlomohle, who visits his father after he has been wounded: 'He was waiting for a blood letting as one anticipates one's first make. Everything that he despised in himself, he hoped, would be cleared and purified completely, after he had carried out, just once, a real action'. This is a Fascist view of killing, seeing it for what it can achieve of itself. But the young heroes of Shamir's early works are not of this ilk. They do not want to kill for enjoyment of it, or fascination with it, or out of curiosity (to see how it acts on their psyche). They are prepared for the kill, a repugnant and horrifying task, because it is a necessary task in the achievement of their necessary purposes.

* *

In my discussion of the central place of youth in these novels of Shamir's, I hinted at the character of the hero. Because the hero was, of necessity, young, and because he had to fight, he had also to be strong. He had to be sure of his views, not to be introspective, divided, tortured, as the Diaspora soul familiar to Jewish experience. He had to fight and die, and he had to be sure of what he was fighting and dying for. It was for his Land, for a small, parched, difficult and problematic Land, but one which was (in his terms) certainly his own. So the contact with the Land, not just as a theoretical construct but as a physical reality, is stressed throughout. There is great play, for example, on the attachment to the Negev in במו ידיו *Bemo Yadaw*. This is seen mystically as more than just a stretch of desert rock, but as the very heart of Israel which is also more than just another country: 'The Land of Israel is occurrence. It is not a place. It is not a collection of places. It is a plant, it is growth which is unceasing, it is rhythm'. Which is to say that it is expressed in a kernel what Israel is about altogether. Everything to do with attachment to the Land is healthy, as we saw above in the description of Willy in הוא הלך בשדות *Hu Halakh Basadoth*: 'He grasped kibbutz life healthily and totally'. The antithesis of this particular thesis is expressed by Avraham Goren in the same novel. He is a fine and admirable person who does much for the settlement. He has attracted Rutti, Willy's wife, away from her husband, perhaps because, amongst other things, he is so totally different from the accepted and desirable norm. But this opposite version expresses precisely the danger of that position. Goren is not totally at ease on the kibbutz, he is not completely at one here. Because 'he has so rich an inner life of his own' he lacks anchor. 'Because he had no root, he was distant and removed. He lived his own life, he read a lot in foreign languages, took little part in general discussions, and would never be appointed to a public function'. The attitudes required for the specific current situation are not these, but rather those which Willy has selected and into which Uri has grown naturally—a sense of total devotion to the common, national cause, sacrifice of one's specific individuality for the general good, persistence, stored courage, collective responsibility. The land is a 'limb of my limbs'. So the hero type of the Shamir novel can now be sketched. He is, although sometimes lonely as is Elik ('here there began to appear in him a nagging feeling of his own loneliness which never left him. Sometimes, it was sharp and clear, sometimes repressed and dimmed, for many days when he was first at the Institution') never actually willing to give expression to his isolation from the group. His responsibility is social, and he accepts it. His loneliness is private and suppressed. He constantly takes action on the social plane, vis-à-vis his family, vis-à-vis his schoolmates, for the benefit of his fellow workers and, above all, for his co-fighters and those under his command in the Palmach. Similarly too, he is attached to the non-human, physical world, to the environment which held the charge of things in themselves. He would receive a sense of mystical union 'in contact ... with essences, with essences that constituted collectively the nature of things around him'. Everything 'had to be touched and felt', because Elik was someone who would thrill intensely at live contact with the physical world. Which all points to the fact that, in spite of various occasional private hesitations and dislocations, Elik, in public life, was other-oriented. As the world, including the narrator in the novels and their readers, see him, Elik acts socially in the public sphere. He acts for the group, and specifically, for the group that he has selected for attachment of his own loyalty, self-identification and affliction.

It seems then that there is an ideology underlying the public activity of the early Shamir hero. There is an acceptance of the particular historical situation as a Fate, self-imposed and enjoyed. The means necessary for the fulfillment of the objects implied by that Fate are welcomed too. His selected group is of primary significance, and since unpleasant means are necessary for the implementation of group purposes, these must be accepted. In order to achieve the national dream, power must be seized. Says Elik, in seeing the exercise of British might: 'The conclusion is in the main; this is what we have lacked, this is what we still have to achieve; power, our own power, independent, not in service'.

* * *

Shamir's technique in these novels is traditional, in the mainstream of the almost straight presentation of a story in palatable shape. For all the various differences of overt subject matter and surface form, there is a great deal of similarity in the composition of these novels; in general tone, in assumption, in scope, in narrative voice and in deeper form. In all three books, the end is prefigured in the title, or from the start, or in the mood. The assumptions are largely those made by one writing in the context of the group—here, the young emergent Israeli society. The scope is the local situation in Palestine/Israel, the kibbutz, the Haganah and Palmach. The tales are told of young men, close to the author's own age, close too to his own experience and view of the world, who fight the good fight, sacrifice their own benefit for the sake of the greater cause which is then carried forward. The narrative voice is a knowing one, both in the sense that the narrator does literally know what is happening in all parts of the story (he is omniscient), and because he knows the thoughts of his protagonists so intimately. These thoughts and assumptions are expressed in a rather generalised way, in the crystallised literary Hebrew usage of the twentieth century. The deeper form transcends incidental differences of technique. The tale is a moral tale; in essence it is very simple. The hero is recognisable, clearly delineated, in common, general outline, in spite of the (again incidental) local shades of stress. The enemy too is clearly marked out, standing in the way like the dragon before St George, hissing and breathing anti-Jewish fire. The task as well is quite simple. The dragon must be slain, so that the maiden Israel may be redeemed. But each individual hero is not an ultimate in himself. If he personally be liquidated, the larger hero, the collective, can pick up the lance and continue the fight.

In this sense, Shamir is writing for the group, and is its representative. The Palmach literature is the expression of the collective—nascent Israel become articulate. For all the immaturity of this literature (and there has certainly been a revulsion against it in current literary fashion), it fulfills an important function in the expression of a society and the feeling of a young force. It is also important in the history of Hebrew literature. The writing of the Palmach generation marks the self-conscious beginnings of a new phenomenon in the world of Hebrew literature, i.e. Israeli literature. The early literature of that generation now seems static. Because it lacked, or deliberately deprived itself of roots in the past, it did not seem to contain the growth potential for the future. So many of the Palmach writers seem to be adolescently fixated. The experience of the group might have been too new and too powerful. It may be too that the writers of that generation were over concerned with the contemporary representation of that experience, and that their efforts to record it were too literal. The heroes of this fiction were adolescent, cut down in their prime. And the fiction might have followed that procedure.

Shamir tried to extend the boundaries of his novel in the period following. From the early fifties on, he looked to Jewish history for the basis of a larger canvas, or for situations parallelling the present: מלך בשר ודם *Melekh Basar Wadam* (King of Flesh and Blood, 1954), כבשת הרש *Kivsath Harash*[1] (Lamb of the Pauper, 1957). He also represented in a later novel the efforts of the character to depart these limits, or this border, altogether, in הגבול *Hagvul* (The Border, 1966). He later however made a renewed attempt at the portraiture of his times and of the local situation, both in political commentary, in, for example, חיי עם ישמעאל *Hayay 'im Yishmael* (My Life with Ishmael, 1965), and in a trilogy attempting to trace the history of the yishuv in novel form, beginning with יונה מחצר זרה *Yonah Mehatzer Zarah* (Dove from Another Garden, 1973). His narrative effort has returned to the groove initially cut in those early novels, to that of the romantic social realism which is both his strength and his limitation.

---

[1] Translated into English as *David's Stranger* (New York, 1964).

4

WHO TELLS THE STORY
IN S. YIZHAR'S *HIRBETH HIZAH*?

In the course of the Israel-Arab War of 1947-9, S. Yizhar (born 1916) produced four stories that reflect the war condition directly, and that were later collected in one volume ארבעה ספורים *Arba'ah Sipurim* 1950. Of these stories, two of them, השבוי *Hashavuy* (The Prisoner)[1] and חרבת חזעה *Hirbeth Hizah* are protest stories, expressing doubts on the part of the narrator/actor in the story about the actions taken on the part of the Jewish leadership and army (to become Zahal on independence) within the specific campaigns discussed. All of these works are in some respects semi-documentary accounts, barely disguising the actuality of the events, although they, are dressed in fictional guise. But in השבוי, *Hashavuy* and חרבת חזעה *Hirbeth Hizah* the first person narrator looks back on a particular event within the war, and takes up a moral, critical stance towards what was done, both what was done by others and what was done (or not done) by himself. Both of them constitute a sort of confessional reflection on an action after the execution of that action. In both stories, a delineated external plot imposes the framework of a furious, self-revelatory reaction on the construction of the story. In both stories, the war is reflected by a participating party, who observes it, considers it, who identifies with the campaign as well as distancing himself from it, and who accepts his responsibility at the same time as he displays total impotence in its regard.

חרבת חזעהי *Hirbeth Hizah* consists of three stages in its plot development: 1) waiting, 2) the action itself (capture of the village, expulsion of the inhabitants and blowing up the houses), 3) the summary (including an embittered self-appraisal as well even as the decision to write the story). It is more complex in construction than השבוי *Hashavuy*, which concentrates entirely on one incident. Here, we have before us the whole process of the capture, with the various incidents that spring from the one operation with all their ramifications. The first stage (the waiting) is shared in common with the first story

---

[1] This story is discussion in Yudkin, *op. cit.*, chap. V.

of the group of four, בטרם יציאה *Beterem Yetziah* (Before Going Out), although in that story, waiting constitutes the total content. Here, it is waiting and everything involved with waiting. Expectation and wistful recollection of the past act as a sharp contrast to the here and now, and cast their shadow on what is going on in the present. Basically, there are various types of waiting: 'Waiting in position, waiting in the course of attack, waiting before going out, waiting during a pause in hostilities; there is the long, merciless wait, there is the excited, turbulent wait, and there is too the totally boring wait, which consumes and burns everything, without fire, without coming to an end, and with nothing else at all'. But this time here, the waiting, at the outset, is seen differently: 'On that splendid winter morning, upon that planted hill, with all around green and irrigated—this was nothing other than a stop on a school outing, when you have nothing to do but have a good time enjoying these wonderful moments and then go back home to your mother'. Not that with this description, the narrator intends to mislead us and feed us with false expectations. He does not want to surprise, because *ab initio* he has prepared us for the unpleasant development. Something terrible is lying in wait; 'Indeed, this all happened some time ago, but since then it has not let go of me'. From the nature of the opening sentence, we can guess the sort of thing that is to come. But even in the light of this recognition, we can also take account of changes in tone in the narrator's reception of impressions, and his record of them. In his specification of the type of waiting in the sharp diversion that then takes place, we see the tendency of the story and its direction. The narrator reveals himself to us from the beginning.

The content of Yizhar's stories is made up of three elements, each of which comes to the fore at a different moment: 1) the 'I' of the story, 2) the group, 3) the landscape. These three things do not exist separately, and there is a reciprocal influence on the part of all over all. The 'I' of the story, whether as first-person narrator or as third-person, a leading figure in the story (or even as a few different figures), shapes the form of the story and establishes its image. In חרבת חזה| *Hirbeth Hizah*, the narrator represents the individual, the conscience that records impressions but finds it difficult to translate the conclusions drawn from his impressions into action. The group is the total body of 'others' that surround the individual. It is true that this group sometimes divides up into separate elements, but these elements only differ in certain external features. The group emerges as contrasted to the individual in its coarseness, its lack of sensitivity and in the immediacy of its needs and desires, as contrasted, too, to the landscape for its very invasion of that landscape, remaining an indigested element. The landscape might be mineral, vegetable, animal or even human (although if human, it is a person who belongs to the landscape and constitutes an inseparable part of it, such as the villagers, the fellaheen, in these stories). The 'animal' also sometimes comes in 'to complete the tranquility of the picture', that is to say, the picture of the landscape. The landscape is ancient. It is there in its proper and natural setting. In this story, the Jewish soldiers are the foreign invaders of the tranquil landscape, whereas the foal remains there after the attack, a remnant of what was, representing, like the horse in a later story הנמלט *Hanimlat*, 'The Runaway' unfettered freedom. Even the soldiers wonder at its appearance, and laud these liberated qualities: 'what wildness, what rebellion!'

The group is spoken of either in the third person plural or in the masculine second person singular, or even in both alternately: 'And when the sun goes round, they fasten a reproachful eye on it and do not move a muscle—that the sun should burst and you should not move. And when eventually a kindly sea breeze blows slightly ruffling and moving the screens of murky dust that hang sultry and angry—immediately there springs up in you a bright expectation, something that— nevertheless. Then with a howl of grief will *you* melt within and they will begin to be reminded of girls'. In this attempt to grasp the generally prevalent feeling, the author goes from '(*they*) do not move a muscle' to '*You* should not move', from 'immediately there springs up in *you* a bright expectation' and 'then with a howl of grief will *you* melt' to 'and *they* will then be reminded of girls'. Those described are the 'they', the unified group, but the 'I' also can belong to them, and sometimes identify with them. The special feature of the 'I' is that he can potentially depart from the framework of the group and react personally and in conscience, in a way not granted to the other.

The landscape is one of the heroes of the story. All are agreed on its beauty. The landscape is the stable element, and the author invests his descriptions of it with a passionate lyrical power. It is this landscape with which the invading foreigner must come to terms: 'And down below, divided by hedges in patches, some extensive and some narrow, marked here and there dark green blobs, rounded off here and there by balls of tree tops, and with hills dotted yellow cast by a host of daisies and with fields ploughed in various places—there crouched the valley at ease, no-one finishes anything, there is no person to be seen, the vegetation of lush lands hums in blue, yellow, brown and green, and by everything between, warming itself in the sun after the rain, turning towards light and to gold and to its heart jumping joyfully, then going silent'. Here is a mixture of description of landscape as it is, memories of the past, and application of the imagination. And through it all, the land-scape is established as a supreme value, something fixed as opposed to the transient. In the end, the landscape must triumph: 'Suddenly, for some reason, the thought occurred that perhaps the path trodden by thousands of steps over generations would soon sprout grass, spoil and put forth fruit with no-one passing by'. The narrator opines more and more strongly during the course of his transmission that the land-scape holds more than can be imagined by mortal witnesses. Following the expulsion, the narrator speaks to Moishe, the group commander, and hears from him that 'new immigrants will come—they will take this land and work it, and it will be lovely here'. The narrator does not react in accordance with these reflections, but he says of the silent village; 'Behind the village starting going quiet piled up with its houses on the hilltop, blocked here and there by trees, out of which the sun had cut out beyond them silent silhouettes, sunk in reflection, knowing much more than us, observing the stillness of the village'.

The reflecting 'I' of the story expresses his concern for the future. Biblical echoes come back to him as an expression of sympathy for those expelled. Soon the village will sing 'the song of the crushing message of sudden disaster which has congealed and remained as a curse not passing the lips, and fear, O Lord, terrible fear cries out from there, and a spark here and there, a sort of spark of revenge, of a challenger, of "God of vengeance appear"'. He poses himself the question of his own guilt. But, in spite of the stirrings of his active conscience, he knows that he must accept such guilt. He is part of the campaign and so belongs to the group. He feels himself split through, even whilst supporting his colleagues at arms, when pointing out the enemy: 'And at that moment, I for some reason shuddered, and with my hand stretched out in drunken enthusiasm in the direction of those running away whom I had discovered, I felt someone shout something else inside me, like a wounded bird, and, still surprised by these two voices' etc, etc. He prays that the soldiers should not hit the escapees, but that does not, in his view, reduce the extent of his guilt.

* * *

In at least one respect, the means employed in Yizhar's stories have also become ends in themselves. The cloak of the Yizhar narrative becomes its content, and one cannot distinguish between them. The stories are composed of contrasts; contrasts between the beautiful and the ugly, between good and bad, between the conscience of the individual and the unfeeling collective, between the will to action and failure to implement. This is all done by use of reflective language. He does this by his five distinctions between types of waiting when he makes distinctions in language that aspires to be the thing itself. He contrasts the day of the task with other days, a summer day for example: 'When it was then noon, so dusty here, winking with moisture of a glossy warmth in the distance, winking and hinting at things, which are, seemingly, not of here, which will not come to you, which boil with the pleasure of a summer day over such a great area, dusted yellow, without shadow, with no possibility of escape, the absolute antithesis of any sort of moisture'. This is nature as opposed to the group. The soldiers reveal complete indifference to life, and their hostility is expressed in their crude argot. The communications officer says to Shmoolik: 'What do you say, see what kind of power the donkey has', and later, 'yesterday I plugged one with three bullets, and he didn't go'. His brutal and ungrammatical language suits his sub-human behaviour. Neither does their attitude to people differ from their attitude to animals. Moishe adopts the most extreme stance, thinking that it would be advisable to finish with the ערבושים, *Arbushim* [2] as quickly as possible. His view is acceptable to others, who then ask him why this has not been done. And the answer: 'Who knows? They've

[2] Derogatory term for Arabs.

decided to be goody-goodies'. Those who express such views are not tough, experienced soldiers but young trainees; '"This isn't war any more, it's a children's game!" delivered himself of this opinion the one sleeping who now stretched himself out, a lad with lovely hair and blonde moustache, a reddish band pulled round his neck in elegant disorder, and it was quite obvious that only a few months ago his mother was telling him off for coming home late'.

The author's language expresses contrasts and comments on them. The whole war brings about a decline of the individual. Almost from the beginning of the story, the narrator notices his own lowering of standards: 'There was a time, when we had just begun to go into the conquered villages, that you still had something delicate about you. One would have preferred to stay standing or to walk around the whole day rather than to sit on this earth, which is not field earth but a rotten patch of dust, fetid and spat upon for generations of people who had urinated and defecated there as had their cattle and camels'. But the language is bound to the external framework, i.e. the recall of an incident that took place, and the individual's reaction following. It does not try to follow the waves of the stream of consciousness.[3] The language serves a clear, specific function—pointed demarcation of contrasts and the expression of psychological shock.

* * *

The story moves on two temporal planes. One is the time of the composition of the story reflecting back, and the other is reported when the events were supposed to have taken place. And this second plane too divides into further layers. The narrator recalls times gone by, as we noted in the description of summer 'when it was then noon' etc., and he projects too into the future. How will the village react when the time comes? It certainly must bear resentment; 'These empty villages, a day will come when they will start shouting. You go through them, and facing you suddenly, you know not whence, invisible eyes of walls, gardens and alleyways accompany you silently. The silence of abandoned desolation'. The tone of the story is

---

[3] See D. Miron's discussion of חרבת חזעה‎ *Hirbeth Hizah* in ארבע פנים‎ בספרות העברית בת ימינו‎ *Arba' Panim Basifruth Ha'ivrith Bath Yameynu* (Tel-Aviv, 1962), p. 351.

established by the dimension of time. Distance reinforces the object of the story and moulds it. It is not written the state of immediate emotion but as a calculated decision, as what is related here is 'one great truth ... and although I am not sure when there is a way out, it seems to me in any case that rather than keep my own counsel, I should in fact tell it'.

The point of view of the narrator is apparently clear. But, just as sometimes the times interchange, so the figure of the narrator becomes blurred. This is what we might expect, as he is ambivalent, indecisive, adopting a stance but then not following through the implications. He shies away from the action, but in fact contributes towards it. He sometimes speaks as 'I', sometimes as 'we', sometimes as 'you' and sometimes as 'they'. He is the narrator, the observer, distancing himself and reporting, the participating soldier, the protesting conscience, and even identifies with those attacked who suffer. History puts him in their place. Here he goes from the 'we' to the 'I'; 'Unawares, it suddenly occurred to me how it was for us, at home, not too long ago, and also longer ago and beyond the recollection of infancy—when there were shots, shots from across the border'. And so he is capable now of self-identifying with the underdog: 'And immediately, seemingly in the same connection, there would appear with precision and certainty ... how they would cross terrified, bowels loose here and there, one mother terrified to death, goes out to gather in her children with the pinching-of-a-heart-almost-stopped. How then is the paralysed silence of astonishment, of "perhaps-not-us, please sir!" so well-known'. So we see that both the time position of narrator and tale, and the point of view of the narrator, match the object of the story. The narrator moves closer and then away, goes from one figure to another, blurs his own presence or accentuates it, as necessary at any given moment.

* * *

This story, like Yizhar's other war stories and like ימי צקלג *Yemey Tziqlag* (Days of Ziklag, 1958) revolves around soldiers, most of them young, prematurely ejected from home. Another contrast that springs to the reader's attention is that between the home background which assumes the dimensions of an idyll, and their present, unpleasant, military situation. Their naive thoughts about girls are far removed from this reality. Shmoolik complains of missing Rivkahle: 'And he passed his hand through the air as though briefly caressing a pretty neck with scented locks falling around, stroking, radiating warmth, then he took and pulled out a cigarette out, lighting it amongst his reflections and a lot of smoke'. His fantasies become more delicate whilst he himself degenerates. He is in his imagination 'caressing a pretty neck' with 'scented locks' at the same time as 'his filthy fingers' hold a cigarette. These soldiers are just children, homesick, imagining a distant warmth. The narrator is party to the sweetness of such yearning. At mealtime: 'We were all smiling, eating, breaking our hunger, passing the time, starting to settle ourselves comfortably. If my ears did not deceive me, the words "back home" kept recurring and your heart would jump at such a wonderful possibility of solution and salvation'.

Such moments act as breaks and offer the opportunity of other possibilities. 'Then' is different, the past is different. Meanwhile, the hard reality comes back. What can be done now other than get quit of the whole business? Moishe explains: 'First we have to go through all the Arabs collected down below and identify young suspects. Then the transport trucks will come along and will load them up and leave the village empty. Thirdly, we've got to finish off burning and blowing up. Then we'll go home'. Here then is an itemisation of the objective, and a sharp about turn takes place in the mood of the narrator: 'For some reason my bowels shrivelled up and I couldn't take the food'. He recalls this horrifying episode, fulfilling his minimal duty in recording the incident in print (see the beginning of the story). That is why he stresses every detail in the disintegration of the collective lives of the Arabs in flight. The story hinges then on the contact of the narrator with a distressing reality, and his reactions: 'I took the field glasses, and then saw them, group after group, maybe family after family, maybe those with equal capacity for flight together, four, five, six, or individuals, also women recognisable by the white scarves on their black clothes, their running, through tiredness and breathlessness, slowed down to a walk, then speeded up once again to a heavy trot, which, more than pace holds the surrender of all powers and breath to proving that everything is done for the sake of running. That they should escape the hand of Fate'. Piling up of words and stress of their significance create a story of offended conscience, a protest story.

* *
*

In this story of clashes, between the 'hero' and the group, between the actual and the ideal, between conscience and reality, there is also an expression of the conflict between the two societies, the Arab society rooted in the land and the interloping Jewish society. Every element of this foreign society expresses such confrontation. The Jewish society is equipped with the latest gadgets whilst the village society remains unchanged since its origins. The narrator is one of the inter-lopers in the vehicle: 'We went along slowly following the deep indentations of the jeep which displayed all its acrobatic capacity in leaping around on all fours within these grooves and all the muck, which after so many peaceful generations of bare feet and asses' hooves, were now forced to suffer silently two scars throughout their length, spitting mud and silence'. The scars created by the vehicle are a wound cut by the enemy in the flesh of the tranquil sufferer. Now, this ancient society will crumble and collapse, and what remains will be just 'remnants of devotion with no base any more'.

It is quite clear from the manner of expression and presen-tation that the narrator is angry about what is going on around him. So, one must ask why he accepts the situation and submits to such a procedure. Here, if such explanation be needed, he explains himself: 'I accept everything and hate feeling different, do not want to be distinguishable in any way from them all. That always ends up in frustration. Every insignificant crack is prised open wider and begins shouting. I took hold of myself and kept firmly quiet'. The narrative, self-revelatory 'I' comes along and solves the problem of the story. Why, if he is so against the way things are handled, does he not intervene to change them, or, at any rate, not participate, or at the very least, express his reservations with greater conviction? In effect, he is pulled in two directions and serves two masters—one, society, with which he seeks to identify: 'I do not want to be distinguishable from ...' and two, absolute justice, his justice. But, also, in effect without raising a finger, he feels weak and estranged. During one of the pauses 'we lit cigarettes, ate oranges, chatted of this and that. And I could well feel how foreign I was, how out of place'. He gets the worst of both worlds. On the one hand, he is not affiliated, and on the other, he does not work for justice.

What, then, is the solution, or, at any rate, his solution? The narrator draws the conclusion of his separateness and impotence, in his own schizophrenia. After he hears Moishe's account of the objective—examining the Arabs, emptying out the village, finishing off the burning down and blowing up, he expresses a 'suppressed desire ... to get up and get right away from here quickly, before the thing begins, and is actually put into effect'. His motivation is not very honourable: 'If it has to be done, let others do it'. It seems that he will not try to stop others doing the dirty work, but he is not ready to soil his own hands. He starts a dialogue with himself: 'But immediately another voice chirped inside me, singing out: delicate soul, delicate soul, with growing irritation and a lilt for the refined soul who leaves the contemptible work to others, who piously closes his eyes and turns them aside to save himself from what might be annoying, such as "see-no-evil", such a "cannot look on iniquity". And so I despised my whole being'. His view of himself moves from gentle mockery to self-hatred. The attraction in opposite directions creates a short circuit, the explosion of the personality, and a split. A similar situation is described in השבוי *Hashavuy* when the narrator has responsibility for the prisoner. On the one hand, he wants to release him for simple humanitarian reasons, and on the other hand, he submits to society's conventions, that society that pressurises him (at least, as he sees it). The result is inaction. And the end 'It is clear that nothing will be. A flash in the pan. Of course, you'll get out of it. You'll ignore it. It is clear that all is lost. Unfortunate prisoner, he hasn't enough strength to act'.

Now, back to the plot. After all, the narrator is supposed to be relating an incident that took place, things that happened, an event that involved the fate of actual people. Here, there is not merely a meeting of societies, but of people who confront each other face to face. What is the image of the Jewish aggressor and the Arab aggressed in the story? The Jewish aggressor reverses his traditional role in history and the Arab aggressed now takes over the function of the wandering Jew known for thousands of years. The Arabs here are all terrified unfortunates who do not know how or why they have been involved in this dreadful episode. Running away from the village, an old Arab asks for his camel, and Moishe puts a simple choice to him:

'Your life or the camels'. Another soldier, Ariyeh, offers to shoot him: "What do you want this turd for? They should get to know that we don't like clever tricks'. In support of this hawkish stand, Aryeh says, 'Imagine a Jew in his place and Arabs in ours. What? They would cut his throat like nothing'. All the soldiers in the group remain under the impression that Jews are 'merciful people, sons of merciful people', and that the Arabs are bloody murderers. The fact that the roles are reversed here has no effect on these mental stereotypes. The Arabs encountered by the soldiers are a representative of the enemy rather than a person with ordinary demands. So the soldier sees him as a symbol and the total apotheosis of evil. The narrator sees these Arabs differently, because he experiences great guilt feelings towards them, and begins to descry certain similarities to the historical Jew (about whom he has only heard from others). He gets into their skin in order to feel what it is like to be them. They are frightened, passive: 'I don't know if they were told before they left where they were being taken, what was expected. In any case their appearance and gestures suggested frightened sheep, terrified, obedient, quiet, sighing, not knowing what to ask'.

The image of the Arab world here also augurs badly for the future. Soldiers blow up the village, and await signs of its destruction. Now the howl begins, though not the sort of howling that is quickly silenced; 'But a howl, a sharp cry, high, obstinate, rebellious, terrifying, continually rising, that you had to hear, that you could not ignore. Impatiently, you shrug your shoulders, look at your friends and want to move on; but this is no longer like the cry of a trapped, frightened chicken, but the shriek of a leopard angered by its pain, receiving an access of evil power, like the shriek of one condemned to the gallows hating and rebelling against the hangman, a shriek that is a defence weapon, a shriek of I-will-not-move, I won't let you, don't touch, till the stones begin shouting'. This shriek embodies absolute confrontation, a watershed in the chain of history. Here something has changed forever, finally. The shriek becomes 'a complaining, rising wail, a hoarse wail, whose power has waned from the sharp shriek, when it is clear that all is lost, finished, nothing will do any good or be changed'. It is possible that it is not known what has been established for the future, perhaps just the fact that something of significance has taken place.

* * *

And if we are speaking here of a historic moment, that is to say, of a moment that will change the face of the world (although, it is true, just of this limited world), what significance can one assign to it? The narrator speaks to one of the soldiers and argues that there is no need to expel the inhabitants from the village. But when asked what he himself would propose in place of expulsion, his answer is woefully inadequate: 'I don't know yet'. He is genuinely uncertain, and so, according to the advice of his colleague, he should shut up: 'It seems that this counsel should have been adopted from the beginning'. But he is not satisfied with silence, and once more, discussion turns on the nature of justice and its relationship to their behaviour. Is there a special war ethic? Do they have to accept in silence everything implied by the concept 'war'? In this context and at the end of the story, the author-narrator brings in the fate of the Biblical city, Sodom, as a point of comparison to what is being done. He starts the discussion with himself with the argument, 'It is always different', and ascribes a far-reaching conclusion to such a point, 'And were those villages that we took in the storm of war also not different? Or those who fled from themselves pushed by fear of shadows? Or the villages of the despoilers for whom Sodom's fate was insufficient—were they not completely different?' Here again he appends to himself the label 'delicate soul', an appellation is not at all postive. The narrator is a delicate soul, i.e. he is afraid of playing a full part, or even of identifying of 'seeing, being, feeling until blood comes' and is afraid too of voicing an explicit protest. So he arrives at self-contempt.

But what is implied by the oblique reference to the destruction of Sodom? It would seem that there is far more that divides than is in common between the two incidents. Firstly, Sodom was destroyed for being evil; Abraham could find no righteous men there. In the case of *Hirbeth Hizah* the opposite is the case. Its inhabitants are innocent, and they are expelled for no sin of their own. Who, then, are the wicked ones, if not the Jewish aggressors? Retribution will come later. Following the shock, God will visit the place. The confusion here stems from the fact that in the Biblical account, God descended on Sodom before destroying it: 'I will go down and see if like its cry to me have they carried out extermination and if not I should know'.

(Genesis 18:21). In the story here, God descends to the village after its destruction and when it is quiet. This is the end of the story: "And when silence closes in on all, and no-one breaks the stillness, and it hums quietly with what is beyond silence—then will God go out and descend to the valley to wander there and see whether it is like its cry'. The similarity perceived by the narrator in the two instances is hinted at by the use of the words (one word in Hebrew) הכצעקתה 'whether it is like its cry', which is the cry of iniquitous violence, a cry which rends the silence recorded by the story. The valley itself cries out at the iniquity already committed, iniquity that cannot be mitigated by new inhabitants. It seems that God's revenge will still come.

* * *

This story deals with a political reality, and will certainly provoke emotional arguments which, in turn, evoke an emotional response. A literary discussion merely looks at the literary evidence, not at the justice of the author, of the narrator or of the characters in the story. חרבת חזעה *Hirbeth Hizah* is a tendentious story that exploits literary tools to reinforce the stand of the narrator as it emerges in the story itself. As noted above, the narrative concern revolves around the question of the justice or otherwise of destroying an Arab village in the course of war, and in expelling the inhabitants therein. The argument takes place in the story, although there can be no doubt as to the narrator's stance. One can also question the weight that is ascribed to the contrary opinion. We are dealing here with a preconceived position. The angry committed narrator deploys a full range of irony in his presentation of the act's justification. If new immigrants arrive, the whole matter is reduced to 'questions of housing and problems of absorption'. Then 'long live the Hebrew Hizah'. Here, we hear a strong note of protest. We have done (and are doing) to our enemies what the Babylonians did in their time. Perhaps there is amongst 'the exiles another Jeremiah, pessimistic and passionate, working up fury within his heart, calling out in stifled tones to an old God, from the wagons of exile'. The narrator is suddenly made aware that 'exile, this is exile. Such is exile. Thus appears exile'. And we are not just looking on as though history is repeating itself in another, new version, but 'we' have brought this about: 'Who will imagine that there was once a Hirbeth Hizah, where we expelled and took over, where we came, shot, burnt, blew up,

66

pushed, drove out and into exile'. Undoubtedly, there are in this dirge echoes of the refrain from the Day of Atonement service, 'We are guilty'. Now, his history lessons assume a new significance. Perhaps we have learnt from history in order to reverse it: 'Wait two thousand years of exile. Whatever not. Killing Jews. Europe. We are the masters now'. Perhaps, in the course of time, the sharpness of feeling will be dulled: 'Both the pain of shame too, and the anger of impotence will turn into a sort of neutral estrangement, shamefacedly disappearing and fading out'. But, even if man forgets, God will not, and we can await His coming for the results of His inspection, His descent and His review.

5

THE HEBREW NOVELIST AND
JEWISH HISTORY: HAIM HAZAZ AND HIS
LITERARY TRADITION

The writing of Haim Hazaz (1898-1972) may, at first glance, appear to be schizoid, or, at least of disparate materials. Its overt concerns are diaspora Jewry and settlement in Israel, the enclosed, traditional world of the Yemenites both in their original homeland and in the Holy Land, and the more sophisticated European communities. But a closer examination does after all reveal a single thread—the Jew and his history. Hazaz's stories, long and short, early and late, as well as his play and his speeches (some of which were collected and published posthumously)[1] revolve around the meaning of Jewish history. The word 'meaning' is used advisedly. The Jewish situation is often grasped by the Hazaz character or 'hero' not as a static subject beyond normal processes, but rather as something which is both capable of change and which might indeed, in a sense, have already been radically altered. The most powerful agent of such change is the Messiah, who will bring redemption. Many of the author's Oriental Jews await the imminent arrival of this figure who is to transform the world in general and the Jewish community in particular. And, on the other hand, the Hazaz figure (here, more typically, the Ashkenazi) has seen in the post-1948 era an actual transformation of Jewish existence in the emergency of a Jewish State. Jewish history in exile was the passive creation of external forces, not a self-authenticating factor. But with sovereign statehood, Israel can again become the subject of history and not just an object. Does this transformation also imply an opposite and so non-Jewish role (in the diaspora sense)? Or, will the Messiah negate previous Jewish history? Is this the 'end of days' (title of Hazaz's play set during the time of Shabatay Tzevi)? Or is redemption, in its sacred or its secular form, only a constant *possibility*, a mental image which can never be actualised, but

---

[1] See משפט הגאולה *Mishpat Hageulah* (Tel Aviv, 1977), where the motto commands 'this generation to stand by for redemption'. Both the motto and the title given to the collection (Sentence of Redemption) testify to the author's recurrent concern in these pieces.

which must always be projected to make life in the present bearable and liveable? Is redemption a figment of the imagination, an internal rather than an external state? History too may be a product of the people's psychology.

These are the questions raised by our author in a literary career which began in 1918, but whose major products spanned the 1940s, 1950s and 1960s. Hazaz's life pattern was so typical of the Hebrew writer of the twentieth century. Born in the Ukraine, he moved to Paris in 1921, and then settled in Palestine in 1931. Like so many other Hebrew writers, he was witness to the very special Jewish Fate with its varying fortunes over the century, both in Israel and in the diaspora. Perhaps untypically, he also took it upon himself to etch a community not so well-known to the world of Hebrew literature, the Yemenite community and, in the broader sense, to record a view or views (not necessarily the author's own) of Jewish history as a whole. His tool was a rich, multi-tiered Hebrew, rooted in the ancient sources and much influenced by the literary renaissance of Yiddish and Hebrew literature of the nineteenth century. Particularly was he influenced by the bilingual writer Mendeli Mocher Sforim and his synthetic Hebrew, but he would also pepper his text where necessary with representation of the dialectical peculiarities of the Oriental communities, with Arabisms and idiomatic idiosyncracies in dialogue.

Such a preliminary outline of this major Hebrew storyteller should not lead us to a view of him as a fictional ideologue, a philosopher manqué, who merely selects an appropriate fictional garb for popular ideologies or historical overview. In the Mendelaic tradition of the Hebrew Enlightenment, and in the East European (particularly Russian) tradition of the writer as the representative, responsible, 'intelligent', Hazaz did make ideas central to the work. As a Hebrew writer too, he placed the Jewish obsession, the meaning of Jewish existence in history, at the centre of the stage. But whatever his faults (and Hazaz is not an easy writer for the current Hebrew reader, who may find his language mannered and self-conscious, and conclusions contrived), our author does not forget that he is telling a story. The idea is there, but it is there to build the character and thus the drama. Hazaz is a writer in love with the language that he uses, selecting choice vocables and phrases redolent of a long life and varied application, but his ambition is to integrate that language into the tale. It is both his overt concern (the subject of his writing) and his tools (the language) that create the effect. This effect is a monument to the Jewish past and to the current struggle, both spiritual and physical. These are stories that require an effort to understand.

* * *

Hazaz, then, is a writer in the East European tradition of Mendeli. He is aware of the linguistic baggage of the past, and he aspires to an interpretation of Jewish existence. He is aware too of the responsibilities of the writer in society (here, within the Jewish community), and he evidently sees himself not just as an entertainer, but as a recorder and messenger too. As a portraitist of the Jewish community, he often describes the general rather than the particular. He consciously seeks out the typical, as though he were a chronicler of precious material on the way to extinction. As at the opening of the story דורות ראשונים *Doroth Rishonim* (Earlier Generations);[2] 'Beloved by me are the hamlets of yesteryear, poor homes of the Jewish community, condemned by generations of writers and commentators, undermined by poetasters and rhymesters, mocked by fools and cleverdicks, enslaved by governments and administrators, breached by bands of brigands and robbers, until they have finally disappeared'. This is a single sentence, portentously composed as a ritual dirge lamenting an extinct but beloved phenomenon. And here we may note a new role assumed by the author. In spite of his appreciation of earlier and contemporary Hebrew writers, and in spite of the fact that he remains clearly and self-consciously within their literary tradition, he still feels that they have done scant justice to their subject matter, i.e. the community of Israel that they have sought to distil. Mendeli, Brenner et al., following the educational line of the Haskalah (Jewish Enlightenment) and perhaps following too the honoured prophetic line, were castigators and reformers. There is sometimes very little love in their descriptions, Mendeli probing with gentle (and sometimes not so gentle) parody, Brenner blasting with frenzied, bitter spleen. But two or three decades later, with all gone in the wake of the First World War, the Russian Revolution and the great migrations, Hazaz would seek rather to erect a monument to a dear departed. Then he sees a different image of the stetl. As he afterwards wrote in

[2] In the volume ריחיים שבורים *Rehayim Shevurim* (Tel-Aviv, 1942).

another context with reference to the limitations of earlier Hebrew writers: '... But this is not sufficient; the stetl did not have just a dark or miserable appearance'.[3] So if he had an educational function additional to those earlier heroes of Hebrew literature, it was to present a more favourable, perhaps more objective image of the Jewish life of yesteryear. Whilst Mendeli and even Brenner were writing about it, they were still involved in a living controversy for the reform of the community, and (at least in Brenner's case) for a radical revaluation of Jewish life. Not so Hazaz, who was from the thirties onwards more concerned rather to induce a greater appreciation of the Jewish past, and then to encourage Jewish efforts towards the concentration of the whole people in Israel. The dialectic of Jewish life was being worked out at this late stage within a different environment. Slavery and redemption were assuming concrete reality, and could be viewed through either a religious or a secular lens.

Mendeli had extracted the typical from the particularities of the world created. In ספר הקבצנים *Sefer Haqabtzanim* (Book of Beggars, published in Hebrew from 1901 onwards)[4] he asserts through his narrator, 'All Jews are beggars', or rather, the community is one big beggar. Which is to say that the essence of Jewish life is parasitism. Hazaz also seeks the characterising generality. But he seeks it through the sort of nostalgia of 'Earlier Generations'. There are loving descriptions of food; Reb Brishel is positively infatuated with the variety of dishes that his wife Perele can prepare for him. This to such a degree that his latter-day desire to go to the Holy Land is shelved when she offers to cook in the Oriental manner. He decides to forego such a diet, and even for that matter the holy soil itself. He simply does not raise the subject again: 'From then onwards, they did not return to the matter of the Holy Land, and Perele wasn't sure if he had been having her on, or if it was her potatoes that had done the trick'. Of course, his wife was relieved that his eccentric notion was dropped so shortly after its original conception. But the portrait of these types and of the total atmosphere is imbued with an aura of love and devotion.

In other contexts too, where the author describes the past, he

[3] *Op. cit.*, p. 32.
[4] This was published in Hebrew from 1901 onwards, but it first appeared in Yiddish as פישקע דער קרומער *Fishke der Krumer* in 1869 and later recast.

conveys a sense of regret at what no longer exists. דלתות נחושת
Dalthoth Nehosheth (Gates of Bronze, 1957)[5] is a novel about
Mokri-Kut, a stetl in the Ukraine, which, although in his view,
had known poverty and deprivation, had still been blessed with
a vibrant Jewish life; 'But if it had not been distinguished by
poperty and wealth, there were still many study-houses, all sorts
of hevrahs, such as a Mishnah hevrah, a Psalms hevrah, a
visiting hevrah, etc'. Needless to say, now everything is
different, because that world is gone. The very language used by
the author indicates regret at the death of that old world. The
new world was heralded by the Bolshevik Revolution, greeted
only by a residue of ignoramuses and poor muts. Descendants
of rabbis and great scholars were now revolutionaries. דלתות
נחושת *Dalthoth Nehosheth* retails the revised situation.

As I have assigned Hazaz a literary place in the tradition of
Mendeli, I should also localise some of Mendeli's techniques, so
that the Hazaz debt could then be identified and its adaptation
be viewed. Mendeli, through his narrator Mendeli the bookseller (an adopted literary pseudonym), aspires to a photo-
graphic representation of the contemporary Jewish scene. Some
critics such as David Frishman[6] even granted this assumption
and asserted that Mendeli's writings were such a faithful
reproduction, and that the Jewish stetl of his time could be
precisely reconstructed on the basis of his literary model. But
Mendelaic technique does not allow this, in terms of the literary
convention adopted. The author works within a framework of
parody and allegory. The bookseller is the ironic observer. The
places observed are ascribed symbolic names, e.g. Kisalon
(Fooltown), Batalon (Idletown), supposedly embodying the
most distinctive qualities of those towns. The narrator's
function as bookseller enables him to travel from place to place,
and draw appropriate conclusions as to the characteristic and
the typical. But that typical is caricatured. This is a perfectly
legitimate technique; caricature is the most potent weapon in
the satirist's armoury. But we must not mistake this technique

---

[5] The edition cited here throughout is the *Collected Works* (Tel-Aviv,
1970).

[6] See his essay 'Mendeli Mocher Sforim' (Warsaw, 1910) in *Collected
Writings*, Vol. 6 (Warsaw, 1930).

for neutral, naturalistic representation. This would be to distort the nature of the beast. All Mendeli's constructs in this vein lead to such an unavoidable conclusion. Parody emerges from the substitution of the grotesque for the dignified or the sacral, where the reader would more naturally expect the latter in a weighty passage. In מסעות בנימין השלישי *Mas'oth Binyamin Hash-lishiy* (Travels of Benjamin the Third),[7] the very title involves daring and achievement. But the actuality there rendered is ludicrous. The Jewish Don Quixote, setting out on his voyage of discovery, is, in fact, an absurd, helpless character, suitably paired with Sendril, his loyal Sancho Panza. They, in fact, hardly move from their starting point. One weak factor in the story (and there are many) is the inconsistency of narrative viewpoint. It is not quite clear whether we are being told the story from within, as seems to be the case from the narrative, (for then we should have it told in good faith without criticism) or from without, about our hero.

Hazaz writes, like Mendeli, in the awareness of recording the typical. But, as we noted above, the satirical intent is considerably reduced. The overtly parodic components, the symbolic names, the allegory, are not so prevalent. And the tone is warm and nostalgic. One short story of his is called simply אדם מישראל *Adam miyisrael* (The Typical Jew).[8] Here is a story within a story related by a pioneer in Palestine, about his father. But even the most specific action of this father, is recorded as representative. This, for example, when he left his family: 'It sometimes happens to a Jew that he has had a surfeit of the world's vanities, and cleaves to the Creator in holiness, enthusiasm and devotion'. Perhaps this sort of action would most typically have been ridiculed by Mendeli, with his demonstrated contempt for unworldliness and for neglect of proper human and social responsibilities. Hazaz interprets the man's action generously and tells his story with warmth. In spite of his extreme poverty, that man was known to distribute charity, in fact, all the money in his possession. Contempt for worldly goods is advocated by many of Hazaz's characters, who are concerned with lasting values and eternal life over and above transient trivia. This man truly seems to exemplify the Jewish spirit. Unlike the Mendelaic pious, he is profoundly

[7] Published first in 1878.
[8] In the volume ריחיים שבורים *Rehayim Shevurim*.

73

joyful in the execution of God's will. The story that the young pioneer tells of his father is really a non-story, or rather a story without a plot. It simply ends with the man's death. After one of his lengthy excursions in the course of the bloody war which particularly hit the Ukrainian Jewish communities, he is slaughtered. They find him with his head chopped off. The author concludes, not with the story within the story, but with his own narrative comment: 'But there is no tale of a Jew these days which does not end in that sort of disaster. And the more you try to conceal such things, the more they emerge'. Which, in sum, means that the author wants here not to relate a peculiar or piquant incident, but rather to grasp the characteristic. This Jew was like so many saintly people. And like so many too in this generation, he was pointlessly murdered. He is a typical Jew, and this was a typical event. For this reason the name of the story indicates its typicality. Just as Mendeli did in his day, so Hazaz, not just here but throughout, points to the generality before arriving at the specific subject of the story. And he might remind the reader at intervals of the story's representative quality. The Yemenites, for example, are selected for treatment in the Oriental stories as one possible community amongst many as in, for example, the introduction to היושבת בגנים *Hayosheveth Baganim* (You Who Sit in the Garden),[9] where a brief survey of the communities is conducted before the narrator's attention alights on this specific group, and then Mori Said is selected as one possible person (true, a very outstanding man) of various such. But the reader is repeatedly reminded of the larger framework.

History implies plot. If it is a story, it must have a direction and a process of unfolding. There must be movement, even progress. So if there is history, man cannot be living within undifferentiated space. For Hazaz, the story that moves on is Jewish history. It takes its origin from the beginning of its peoplehood, has moved through a certain course of events (mostly unhappy, involving exile and suffering) but it also concomitantly looks forward to a certain development. The object of history in traditional Jewish terms is redemption through the Messiah; the Messiah will mark a radical crux and

[9] First published in 1944.

reverse. Exile will come to an end, as too will Jewish and all human misery.

In religious terms some see the establishment of Israeli statehood as 'the beginning of redemption'. Hazaz's characters in works written before statehood sometimes view the process of the ingathering as a significant step on the way to the Messianic era. Because naturally there is no general agreement on how this era is to be achieved, what it will look like, what sort of backdrop it will have, what sort of person the Messiah will be, or particularly in secular terms, if the Messiah will be simply a person, a lineal descendant of King David, as traditional Judaism has it. But well before the modern period, and particularly during times of travail, Messianic hopes have run high. Hazaz can find such times interesting because presumably of a certain parallel sense with our own. After great suffering perhaps there will emerge the contrast. Are these the 'pangs of the Messiah' so much projected in the sources?

And so his play בקץ הימים *Beqetz Hayamim* (At the End of Days),[10] is set in such a historical period. Significantly, it was written after the rise of Hitler to power and with a sense of foreboding for the dire fate of the Jews. But it was also composed before the declaration of Israeli independence. These two events may be perceived not only as temporally connected but also as causally interrelated. Perhaps if not for the destruction (*hurban*), there would have been no statehood, the ultimate of ingathering that made national redemption more plausible. Religiously, this turn of events could have been seen as embodying God's action in history. Secularly, these developments could mark a reversal of Jewish history, perhaps a summation, perhaps a peak, perhaps even its termination in the form that it had been known for two thousand years. In either case, something of massive significance occurred for those involved with the Jewish situation.

בקץ הימים *Beqetz Hayamim* is set in seventeenth century Germany. The background is the rise of Shabatay Tzevi to popularity throughout the Jewish world. Messianic expectations are rife in the wake of the Khmelnitsky pogroms of 1648-9. The play's debate revolves around Tzevi's claims to Messiahship. There are implications too for immediate conduct, because normative Jewish law is nullified after this crux is

---

[10] First published in the journal *Moznayim* (Tel-Aviv, 1935).

achieved. The Messiah changes history, and reverses traditional behaviour patterns. Such antinomian conclusions are drawn by Yuzpa, who asserts that 'the world is to be redeemed by sin'. Yuzpa's wife quotes his view that a 'new heaven and new earth will be created'. This is the sort of eschatological terminology of various Jewish and Christian apocalypses, from the Book of Daniel through the Book of Revelations and later mystical texts. All earlier norms are questioned, because history has radically changed direction. Even sin is to be recreated as non-sin: 'Everything that exists is to be negated, each fence to be breached to pave the way for redemption! To descend to the abyss—that is the teaching of redemption. To love sin—that is the need of the hour'. Of course, this is not the only view propagated. And, as we know from the actual events of the time, the Jewish world was divided precisely over the issue of whether redemption had come or not. One suggestion made in the play by a non-Jew was that even without redemption the Jews should still go ogg to the Holy Land and set up a state of their own. The Rabbi in the play asserts the validity of the halakhah (Jewish Law); he is sceptical of current claims.

So there are three views. One is the assertion of the Sabbatian claim, the second is a refutation of it, and the third offers a consequence of the claim (resettlement of the Jewish people in the Holy Land) without the supporting substance (coming of the Messiah). A debate takes place between Yuzpa and the Rabbi. The Rabbi indeed reaffirms the twelfth of the traditional thirteen principles (originally formulated by Maimonides) that the Messiah will come. Yuzpa asserts on the other hand that the Rabbi does not want to accept the actuality, and only stresses that 'he tarry'. Can the potential be actualised? Both seem to hold to the literal possibility. The question mark hangs over the present moment. Yuzpa then proceeds to a further point which would remove the decision from God's exclusive power: 'Redemption depends on us'. So he introduces a new dimension: redemption as a psychological state. It seems that the Jews do not want to be redeemed. As he says, 'Exile is bone of our bones and spirit of our spirit, redemption is a nice dream that is alright for exile'. Yuzpa's conclusion is that the Jews want to retain grasp of two things, one—the possibility of redemption, two—that it will never come about. Or, to formulate it as a single entity, they believe in the eternal possibility of redemption. The play ends in an orgy of destruction. The poor literally burn the exile, which is henceforth abolished by decree. So they fulfil Messianic expectations and satisfy their own need of revenge.

* *

Much space has been devoted to Hazaz's apocalyptic understanding of Jewish history past and present. He has portrayed Messianic yearnings and Jewish psychology in the seventeenth century, and transferred them to the contemporary scene in היושבת בגנים *Hayosheveth Baganim* where the highly respected Mori Said, now in Jerusalem with the Second World War raging outside, pronounces and lives his conviction of imminent redemption. We are immediately aware that such conviction would not travel easily to a more Europeanised environment of the same period. Hazaz is unusual amongst Hebrew writers in attempting to write at length and in depth about two very disparate kinds of people. The Ashkenazim and Yemenites in his contemporary Israel differ in background, in level of expectation, in life style, and thus too in outlook and belief. And yet, in his portrayal of both communities he highlights his concern, i.e. the meaning of 'redemption' in Jewish history. Some of Hazaz's most potent effects are obtained, from a justaposition of two characters from these two different worlds, each expressing his own world view in his own language. The drama is then played out against the backdrop of current Jewish events. They might even come to similar theoretical conclusions, although they would give them expression in different ways. Such a story is רחמים *Rahamim* (in ריחים שבורים *Rehayim Shevurim*), which, like so many of our author's stories, does not contain a developed plot, so much as the germ of a situation and the expression of character contrasts. The story is simply a meeting of two individuals. One, Menashke, is thin, sickly, tired and feels himself a failure in all respects. He is not at peace in the world, and is not only personally frustrated but also generally resentful of various external forces. The other, who chances upon him walking along in Jerusalem, presents a very different picture, contented though impoverished, as he rides slowly on his ass. They seem to come not only from different backgrounds, but also from different eras. Rahamim the Kurd (as he turns out to be) is very forthcoming, and in his primitive Hebrew he offers practical advice to the other. He must get married. As much as Rahamim reveals himself, so does

77

Menashke conceal himself (although the author does permit glimpses of an unhappy past). Each character, in fact, sees into the other's life. Rahamim tells how he got to Palestine. Menashke, through his demeanour and his limited conversation, hints at the source of his frustration. Rahamim goes his own way after repeating his advice about marriage, but then returns to offer consolation, 'God will have mercy'. Menashke's mood changes only through memory of Rahamim's smile. It seems that the price of sophistication and high expectation is discontent.

Two people, likewise of disparate backgrounds, are brought together in a more sustained manner in the novel בקולר אחד *Beqolar Ehad* (In One Noose).[11] This is set in Palestine during the last days of British mandatory rule, when the Jewish nationalist movements in their efforts to remove the British, wage war against them. Two men under sentence of death await execution in the death cell, Menahem Halperin, an Irgun man and Eliyahu Mizrahi of Lehi. But however different their background, their object was identical. More specifically, they had the same vivid consciousness of the present vitality and relevance of Jewish history. It was still alive for them. 'Those far-off things which happened thousands of years ago were nearer to them than things which happened within their parents' lifetimes a generation earlier'. Nevertheless, a similar difference of temperament is perceptible between the two here to the case in רחמים *Rahamim*. Eliyahu the Oriental is at ease with himself and with his behaviour. Menahem is melancholy: 'Jealousy of him (i.e. Eliyahu) stirred in his heart, that he was so strong, that he was so tranquil, that suffering was put aside, that his thoughts did not weary him, and that they allowed him to sleep'. Here again, there appears the contrast between the two world views, the naive and the sentimental (Schiller's distinction). These are the two representative types of Jew, both, in the author's view, acting authentically and arriving at a single conclusion expressed in action. But the European sophisticate is uneasy, unhappy, full of the dread of the future, in this case, of the death that is imminent. The other, the Oriental, is distinguished by a full acceptance of his role. What is the difference? It may be 'that faith is still with him in its entirety, consciously and unconsciously, in all his two hundred and forty

11 Tel-Aviv, 1963.

eight limbs, as with all his community'. But Menahem has lost all that. He is estranged from his community. And the implication here is that just as Eliyahu is typical of his community so Menahem is the type of the western emancipated Jew, alienated, embittered and removed from the social and communal context.

This is a secular novel set in modern times, but the recurrence of motifs sets Hazaz's central concerns before us. Just as Yuzpa in בקץ הימים *Beqetz Hayamim* accused the Jewish world of being unwilling to accept redemption, so Menahem berates Jewry. It does not want redemption. Here, redemption is not to come in the guise of a seventeenth-century Messiah, but it still can only come if it is wanted. Unfortunately, the Jews, argues Menahem, want 'the dream to continue, to remain unfulfilled. The solution is ... fear, despair ...'. Jewish history is seen by Menahem as a psychological phenomenon. The Jews have invited their fate. Redemption will not be theirs, because unconsciously they reject it. The typical position of Jewish history is that of the *aqedah*, the sacrifice (which could have taken place) by Abraham of Isaac. Menahem recalls an episode to Eliyahu when his father was beating him, and he invites him to 'slaughter me as Abraham slaughtered Isaac'. But the father argues that Abraham was stopped by the angel. 'It would have been better if he had slaughtered him', said Menahem, 'better than always living with the memory of his father over him with a knife'. And since then, the Jews have been like Isaac going to the slaughter. Even now that God does not exist (in the heart of man), they still go to the slaughter without knowing why. The unresolved question is whether this characteristic posture on the part of Isaac will remain unchanged in the wake of the new national development. Eliyahu believes in the possibility of change. That possibility is in the Jews' own hands: 'When someone moves decisively in the direction that he has set for himself—then he is a free man'. One defines one's freedom existentially; fate has the shape of the will. So in a sense does the fate of these two prisoners who refuse to accept foreign (British) authority, who even refuse them the possibility of execution. They blow themselves up in their cell after Eliyahu has devised a plan to secrete bombs into their possession. Characteristically, the author notes that even in death, Eliyahu's countenance bears the marks of repose and Menahem's of discontent. Their own shapes are fixed through the very moment of extinction.

There are psychlogical differences between them throughout, marking the same action with a different accent.

* * *

A fiction writer whose subject is ideologies or history is not thereby a philosopher or a historian. Though his subject may be of theoretical interest and may be too his consuming passion, he still has to shape his material suitably and integrate it into his fiction. We have seen some of Hazaz's concerns and the way that he treats them. But he is not to be simplistically identified with any specific protagonist, statement or ideology presented in the work.

One of Hazaz's stories has become so well-known that it is easy to make a casual substitution of the author for the point of view presented. הדרשה *Hadrashah* (The Sermon),[12] like so many of Hazaz's stories, does not have very much external action or plot development outside of the 'sermon' itself. Yudka, not normally given to public statement, makes a speech to the Haganah [13] Committee. It is what he says that constitutes the major content of the story. But we must not forget that it is (within the literary convention) Yudka's statement not the author's, and, for all the paucity of plot, it remains inside the story. The burden of Yudka's 'sermon', broken as it is by interruption and hesitation, is highly reminiscent of the views quoted by Hazaz elsewhere. What he brings to the committee (as they think, irrelevantly) is a view of Jewish history. The committee awaits some sort of announcement, but Yudka starts off by saying that he does not understand what 'we' i.e. the Jews, are doing in Palestine. He later amplifies the point by saying that he is 'opposed to Jewish history', that he does not 'respect it'. When he is called to order and requested to keep to the issue, Yudka argues that without history we cannot manage the present. He opposes Jewish history because it is not authentically Jewish, i.e. created by Jews. Others have been responsible for the Jewish Fate in Exile. The pattern has been entirely negative, suffering determined by the world outside. It is not even a story of heroism, because such a role has been externally imposed. The Jews have not even rejected suffering;

[12] In אבנים רותחות *Avanim Rothehoth* (Tel-Aviv, 1946).
[13] The word *havurah* (group) is changed to *haganah* (defence forces) in the revised collected edition of Hazaz's writings 1968-1970.

80

they seem to have welcomed it (Menahem argues a similar case is בקולר אחד *Beqolar Ehad*). So existence has become for Jews an other-worldly dream, and a 'nocturnal psychology' has been created, differing from the normal, healthy, day-time psychology of other groups of people. Belief in redemption, in the Messiah (see בקץ הימים *Beqetz Hayamim*), is tolerable and required, as long as such redemption does not come.

If this argument is valid, argues Yudka, what we know as Jewish existence, is the product of this Jewish psychology, and is an Exile existence. Our homeland, Eretz Yisrael, presents its opposite. Zionism, then, is not the fulfilment of Judaism, but rather its very antithesis: 'When a man can't be a Jew, he becomes a Zionist'. The return to Israel is the very negation of Judaism, Hebrew the negation of Yiddish, traditional Jewish names and means of expression are rejected. Yudka reiterates the familiar argument that Zionism and Hebraism are intended to reverse the traditional Jewish role.

The hero of the story does not offer a way out of his dilemma. His speech ends as abruptly and unexpectedly as it starts. He himself feels that he has not said what he intended. He then requests the chairman's permission to start again. But meanwhile the tension is broken, and the audience is prepared to listen. The chairman lets him go ahead, although, as he instructs, 'without philosophy'. There the story ends, and we will never know what he was going to say. But the relief of the audience perhaps indicates a forthcoming retraction. What was said aroused great unease, but now a number of uncomfortable revelations can be reburied.

'The Sermon' is a story, and is created with the tension of a story. The familiar notions are like currants in a cake, certainly vital, but not isolated. Hazaz has used notions of Jewish history and Jewish existence, which clearly give rise to general concern and particular unease on the part of his heroes and narrators. Facile resolution is not offered, nor are the logical conclusions drawn from the views of such as Yudka and Menahem. An implication could be the rejection of Jewish existence, so negative, so unpleasant, so 'nocturnal'. Perhaps the people should come to an end. Perhaps Zionism constitutes a respectful burial, one which could be more discreetly carried out by assimilation. Such possibilities peep out of the statements made by the author's protagonists. But the overall framework of the individual play, story, novel or speech of Hazaz suggests otherwise. There is a problematic dialectic in this oeuvre, but its existence must testify to a stand contrary to its own negation. Nothing is simple. Literature is not philosophy; it is something which creates its own dynamic. The work of Hazaz refutes the material that it has produced.

6 CHARACTER AND PLOT IN THE NOVELS OF YEHUDA BURLA

The Hebrew tale is as old as the Bible itself. Men have always told of the fortunes of themselves and others, of their adventures, their development, and of the way they have become what they are. The Bible opens with an account of the origins of our world, and of the first people on Earth, of the struggle between God and man, between right and wrong. Mediaeval Hebrew literature too revelled in the moral tale, often told in the Arabic style *maqama* of rhymed prose. And in modern times too, many novelists have set the tale at the heart of their work.

Such a writer is the Jerusalem-born Hebrew fiction writer Yehuda Burla (1886-1969), who was productive for about half a century from the outset of the First World War. Prose writers have to a great extent reappraised form and matter, have evidenced scepticism in regard to character and plot, and thus have perceived a need for formal innovation. But Burla has persisted throughout with the traditional tale about men and women perceived as 'characters' affected by life's circumstances, and sometimes changing in respect to these circumstances. Burla's novels always have a hero at the centre. The hero is placed in a setting which arouses conflict, and this conflict is often between his inclination and his environment. Events occur which proceed from the conflict and influence the hero on his life's journey. And the climax, whether disastrous (as in עלילות עקביה *Aliloth Aqavyah*) or conciliatory (as in נפתולי אדם *Naftuley Adam*) points up the nature of the conflict within the individual described. This is life's journey described in the traditional picaresque manner.

It will be seen then that Burla's writing is a little out of joint with its time and place. Hebrew prose had become very experimental in the early twentieth century; Gnessin had produced a new type of impressionistic, introspective language, Brenner had attempted to match the modern condition with a Hebrew that bore the contours of a stream of thinking and awareness, Agnon had produced narrative innovation in line with some European masters. Burla's language is the literary Hebrew of the past centuries (later, with בעל בעמיו *Ba'al*

83

Be'amaw, it becomes more Mendelaic), the picaresque nature of the narrative makes it a recognisable heir to mediaeval forebears. True, there is a concern with psychology, particularly with the conflict noted above. But there is no attempt to render the unconscious through the medium of 'stream of consciousness' through linguistic innovation or through a newly-wrought syntax. Neither, in terms of its subject matter, is the Burla novel the specific product of the twentieth century. The psychological data are more appropriate to the nineteenth century, and the conflict etched is not between a tradition and the modern predicament in the era of Marxism, psychoanalysis, positivism and the disintegrating religious certainty. It is the conflict known to earlier times between authority and personal instinct (עלילות עקביה *Aliloth Aqavyah*) or between social environment and a more personal type of religious view (נפתולי אדם *Naftuley Adam*). To the mainstream Hebrew reader, Burla's subjects were mostly unfamiliar—the Arabic or Ladino-speaking hero without intellectual sophistication, the observant Jew from an Islamic environment, the social assumptions of the East (the place of women, for example). Burla's literary ambition did not alter much in the course of his career, and it remained on the fringes of the literary mainstream of a Hebrew literature predominently shaped by European exponents of the genre and the new Israeli consciousness.

The Burla story typically plunges straight into the action and the central theme. There is an obsession with sexual desire in the face of society's constraints. Even when the desire appears to be fulfilled, some breach (even if minor) of social norms exacts its vengeance. Burla's very first story, לונה *Luna*[1] is a case in point. Here, the brother of a deceased landlord comes to Jerusalem to see his property. One of the tenants, Luna, a young, nubile girl, attracts the attentions of the older, married man. He, Obadiah, argues that monogamy is not a typically Jewish practice, but rather a debased Ashkenazi custom, imitative of the European. He, as a Sephardi (Bucharan), can ignore it, and take a new wife. This he fully expects to effect his revitalisation. So his motivation is clear. His life has turned stale but he is as libidinous as ever and would like nothing more than legitimate fulfilment. What, however, is Luna's motivation? She, at twenty-four, already thinks that life has passed her by,

---

[1] It was actually composed in 1914 but published only after the war.

feeling 'like someone seeing his friend suck something sour in his palate, whilst his own mouth remains empty. His soul is empty, empty yet demanding'. She is fatherless, and her impoverished mother can offer no dowry. So the inevitable marriage takes place, and disaster immediately ensues. Obadiah turns out to be not as wealthy as was thought, and, more importantly, is mean and inconsiderate. Hitherto, Luna had been unfulfilled, but now she is desolate because she no longer has any expectation of improvement. She has a father rather than a husband, and a very unpleasant father at that. He too is disappointed, with her arrogance and irritation. They have to split up, especially as his first wife suddenly makes an appearance. Even though she is pregnant at the time of the prospect of separation, Luna feels victorious and trustful in the future.

This plot illustrates some of the author's preoccupations. The social context is Oriental, but within that blanket term are contained divisions. He is a long-standing Palestinian of Bucharan origin and she is newly arrived from Istanbul (Ladino-speaking and of higher social status). In spite of what appears to be a propitious basis for a marriage that would satisfy both parties, the seeds of conflict are sown *ab initio*. Their expectations are as different as their ages. He seeks respect and loyalty, she romance and excitement. His ways are set; her life is just starting. So with the difference of perspective emerge disruption and disaster. The plot could be summarised as two expectations unfulfilled. Both expectations are based on actual, current, psychological need. But this need drives out wider considerations, long-term, social and communal. The wider context then mitigates against the action taken by the individual in search of immediate satisfaction. Such is the nature of the Burla story, based on the data of 1) inherent character, 2) dissatisfaction, 3) search, 4) solution, 5) retribution and 6) crisis. Obviously, as we shall see, not all the ingredients are identical in all the stories. The plots are as different as their settings. But always, we do get a development of this sort. The Burla story is the story of the character in action. The time scale is often large (frequently a life story of many decades is covered), the setting moves (Syria, Iraq, Anatolia, Palestine—country, town), the hero is of various hues—vicious (אשתו השנואה *Ishtho hasenuah*), adventurous (עלילות עקביה *Aliloth áqavyah*), simple (בלי כוכב *Beli kokhav*), sophisticated (נפתולי אדם *Naftuley adam*), but he is

85

always perceived in this narrative way. The work moves along these narrative stages, although the resolution may be different. This resolution comes from conflict which emerges from the datum of character.

* *

Basic to the Burla story then is character—character perceived, drawn, invoked, described. The author is not detached from the narrative voice nor from the chief figures in the stories.[2] The heroes of the novels are variations on each other. They vary in appearance, apparent temperament and talent. But these are external features easily changeable. Their motivation is, in each case, very similar. They are people (usually men) of great sexual appetite and a nagging ambition which turns out to be insatiable. The author does seek a series of disguises. In בלי כוכב *Beli Kokhav*, for example, the narrator introduces a sub-narrator who tells the story, and the sub-narrator is, unusually, an Arab. נפתולי אדם *Naftuley Adam* is a story told within a story, and the reader is constantly reminded of this artifice. It is, within the terms of that story, told at one long sitting, so the teller (Rahamu) interrupts himself at intervals to check on the audience's attention and comfort. But these devices are irrelevant in the characterisation, which is of a single hue, internally consistent and continuons. And where we have an omniscient narrator, we are still presented with the hero's point of view.

And this point of view finds it difficult to reflect on itself. An early work, אשתו השנואה *Ishtho Hasenuah* (His Hated Wife, 1920), looks back from a contemporary vantage point to the earlier life of the hero Daud Hadad. This is a man who has made good materially, but who is constantly dissatisfied and increasingly miserable. We can see the causes of his misery in an unsuitable marriage principally engineered by his mother. But his motivation is obscure. Why did he not divorce his own wife? Why does he accept his mother's selection? What exactly does he want? These are the unanswered questions that strike the reader. But Daud himself is incapable of even the beginnings of self-analysis. The dissatisfaction is a fact, necessarily there, but

---

[2] See G. Shaked's article המספר לפי תומו 'Hamesaper lefi tumo' in Y. Burla: מאמרים על יצירתו Ma'amarim 'al Yetzjiratho, ed. A. Barshai, (Tel Aviv, 1975).

inexplicable. He has an instinctive knowledge of his own nature, but he seems impotent to act in accordance with it. He knows that he will not be happy with his destined spouse: 'I won't hate her but neither will I love her as a wife', and yet he goes ahead with the marriage. And although the novella covers a thirty-year span of his life these data are neither susceptible to change nor to further investigation. It is as through his primordial fate has doomed him. He is possessed by a great lust particularly for the women of other men. As so often in Burla's stories, the hero has a wise confidant, here, one Haim Sasoon, who reads his palm and pronounces, 'You must overcome the evil inclination—this above all'. This evil inclination drives him on to desire what is not his and to reject his own. It also incidentally leads him to reject Sasoon when that man's fortunes decline. The given character does not develop; we only see further potential for selfishness and self-inflicted misery deepen. Daud does not possess the tools for his own correction nor for his own understanding. He sees his misery as his Fate and his misfortune as retribution for his misdeeds and evil thoughts. That is his religious sense.

So אשתו השנואה *Ishtho Hasenuah* is a limited work, i.e. it does not take us beyond the primary assumption of inherent character. Action plays upon this character, but does not ripen it in the course of the narrative time. This feeling is enhanced by a further datum, the inarticulacy of the hero. The resolution is a sort of coming to terms with his situation; 'so it is wanted in Heaven'. Nothing more. This utter, literally inexpressible bleakness, here unrelieved, is modified in other of Burla's stories. Sometimes, the conflict between society norm and personal aspiration is made explicit. And sometimes too, the hero can articulate the conflict and assess the competing virtues of opposed claims. בעל בעמיו *Ba'al Be'amaw* (A Substantial Man, 1962) presents the author's favourite type of hero, Gideon, physically attractive, strong, adventurous, with unarticulated yearnings. Unsatisfied with following in his father's footsteps as grave-digger, he wants to be a shepherd. That is his first resistance to social pressure. But far more serious is his love for a Muslim girl. Which is to prevail, his personal predilection or the constraints of his society? Gideon can express the problem, and exhorts himself to display resolution and individuality: 'Rise against them ... defend your love with determination, hold yourself erect against them like a mighty rock ... don't be dismayed ... if no-one has pity on you, on your love, or your life, you should have no pity on anyone. Don't submit, don't be like them, like those who love useless loves'. There are two sorts of values proposed here, which take the form of two opposed sources of pressure. And the hero makes his point so strongly that the reader might be persuaded to predict a victory for his individualism over the external group pressure. But the opposition from the two families is overwhelming, both the Jewish and the Muslim. Gideon is persuaded into what he thinks is a compromise—that he should meanwhile marry someone else, and then, years later, after his beloved Hamda has converted to Judaism, he should take her as his second wife. This last possibility becomes increasingly far-fetched, but in the course of years, the couple take on Hamda as a living-in maid. After the prolonged, irregular and unsatisfactory affair, Gideon puts the original conception as a suggestion to his wife. But it is too late. In a series of confidential and complicated events, Hamda disappears.

The author does not normally evince much detachment from the active participants in the story. Even rarer is it to see the hero or events described from another point of view. But we do get something of that at the conclusion of בעל בעמיו *Ba'al Be'amaw*. In his search for Hamda, Gideon hears from her mother, and we now witness what it has been like for her (and for them) over these years: "All these days we have seen in her changes, madnesses, troubles. Now apparently she is fed up with herself and with everything else. Apparently, she has suffered enough. At last, it seems, her conscience has stirred and she has run off'. There is not just one party to the tragedy. We see now that havoc has been wrought on another group of people. Perhaps for the first time too, Gideon's perspective is enlarged so that he can see the implications of his behaviour for others when he admits that 'he has never felt so ashamed as he felt at the words of Hamda's mother'. In an earlier novel, נפתולי אדם *Naftuley Adam* (Man's Struggles, 1929)[3] a similarly forbidden love is proposed. Neither Jewish man nor Muslim woman is afraid of the consequences. But disaster ensues, as her relatives, in bloody revenge, attack and blind Rahamu. The rest of the story, as retailed by Rahamu years later, is concerned with his attempt to reconcile himself to his situation. This he

---

[3] Published in English with the title *In darkness striving*, Tel Aviv, 1968.

eventually manages. But the incident, with its antecedents and its consequences is relayed solely by himself from his own (indeed wavering) angle. The narrative and psychological perspective is focused through a single lens.

* *

This is the manner of Burla's writing—the psychological perspective and the narrative voice. There is a lack of distance between author and narrator, or between the narrator and his characters, as there is also little variety within the story that might offer a rounded view of the events described. So too, there is little ironic distance between the narrator and the narrative, where he might stand back and take a look at himself and his story so as to assess his part in events and make some sort of judgment, even if it turns out to be a wrong one. A rare instance of such irony comes up mildly in the account of Gideon's contrived courtship, in בעל בעמיו *Ba'al Be'amaw* with Sarina Garsani. One of the obstacles to marriage from her family's point of view is his occupation of shepherd, or, at least, its overt expression in shepherd's garb. Gideon has to change his clothes to become acceptable to the urban sophisticates. But the narrator observes the significance of such as adaptation for Gideon: 'Gideon's change of garb after the engagement, which for other people and even for the bride's family, might have been an external matter, was, for him, an inner, a symbolic change'. We assume that Gideon knows that he has now become different, and the narrator (as well as the reader) indicates a transition in life style from the individualistic pastoral to the conformist urban. This is one of the few instances in Burla's writing where the significant resonance echoes beyond the realised scope of the hero himself.

But for the Hebrew reader, much of the immediate interest of the Burla story emanates from the subject matter treated and the outlook of the characters. Such material is understandably exotic for the contemporary Hebrew sensibility which is normally attuned to an Ashkenazic, Western voice. The environment is Oriental, the setting Anatolia, Syria, Iraq, or Jewish Palestine amongst the Eastern communities. The central character is usually a man, and the female role is subsidiary to the male, trying to satisfy, modify and direct his lust, and provide a stable basis for his dynamic thrust. There is much concern with successful male issue to continue the line, and the taking of a second wife is always a possibility, if frequently a problematic one. Success in life is measured by material possessions, by a good family life, by sound male issue, by moral, religious and ethical reputation, and thus, *in toto*, by one's standing within the conforming community. This is the backdrop against which the individual functions, and the Burla hero is often successful in terms of the application of such tests. But the plot of the Burla story derives just from the tension between the individual and his environment, because the individual (perhaps by definition) is not content to be limited by the social context. This context can act as a constraint on his appetite (often undefined), on his unorthodox religious sense, on his inarticulate craving for the ineffable. And strangely enough, this sort of tension is perceptible for the two types of hero—the unpleasant negative, miserable, inarticulate character (from אשתו השנואה *Ishto Hasenuah* for example), or the outgoing likeable, positive, eloquent character (as in נפתולי אדם *Naftuley Adam*). Although the reader may tend to sympathise with one more than another, the nature of the conflict is identical. It is the individual resisting social pressure, martyred in his resistance but miserable in conformity.

The apparent source of dissatisfaction is frequently with the women in the hero's life. But it would be difficult to say whether Eros is the root of the dissatisfaction, or just the overt expression. We have observed a similar phenomenon in both types of hero—the harsh, repressive Daud of אשתו השנואה *Ishto Hasenuah* and the delightful, popular Akaviah of עלילות עקביה *Aliyoth Aqavyah* (Deeds of Akaviah, 1939). But whereas in the first case, the reader may be inclined to favour the dictates of society—after all, his wife is submissive, good natured and brings him luck, whereas he is morose, inexplicably evil-tempered and bloody-minded, in the second case, the matter looks different. No longer can the conflict be seen singly as between good and evil. Akaviah is manifestly concerned with the welfare of his fellow humans, Armenians and Muslims as well as Jews. He is able to justify the ways of God to man and so comfort the sorrowful with his early belief in the eventual coming of the Messianic era. And the reader too may be enchanted by his attraction to the outside, to the open spaces, and the world beyond the immediate confines of his own experiences. Akaviah, like other Burla heroes, has yearnings which he does not understand. As he says to his worried father,

'What secrets do I have? But I don't know how I can say what I have to and what I should say—so I will keep silent. Do I myself know my problem'? He only knows that he lacks something: 'Something is missing in me, and I don't know what'. It is after this expression of the lack (although there remains the inability to articulate its real nature, if indeed there be such) that he meets the great love of his life, the Armenian girl Anaheit—the 'strange fire', the forbidden fruit. In the earlier novel too, Daud does not evince discontent only at the outset of his disastrous marriage. He seems to be born with that characteristic. He too had been attracted to the great 'beyond' and had been trained to look away and rather focus his attention on the more mundane and specific personal concern: 'Daud made an effort to remove his glance from the great expanse, multifarious in appearance and splendour, and to concentrate on and be concerned with his own affairs'. It is then that he is persuaded by his mother to take the bride of her choice. She is to decide his Fate. And it is in Daud's submission to his mother's will that we perceive the surrender of the individual to social (or outside) pressure.

At least in these two works, it is the dissatisfaction that is primary, and the Eros that is the concrete expression of that dissatisfaction. Certainly such is the case in chronological terms. For Akaviah, the meeting with Anaheit brings about not only a great attachment and focus for his love, but a total spiritual reorientation. Since his love must needs challenge social convention, one or the other must be wrong. For him now, God is in the girl. But in spite of his absolute conviction, the social pressures on both parties are again too powerful to allow fulfilment of love which is a merely personal predilection. In a rather strange (and arbitrary) substitution for Anaheit, Akaviah falls in love, after imigration to the Holy Land, with Diamante, a girl bearing a great resemblance to his first beloved. But this new attachment has even more disastrous consequences than the earlier one. His religious sense is revolutionised. He ceases to believe in the Providence of God: 'There is no justice and no judge ... now it is clear to me that God is in Heaven and man is on Earth'. His new religious ecstasy produces Messianic fantasies in Diamante who loses her sanity. Akaviah proceeds, as he says, to leave the sphere of God.

We have already seen a similar conflict expressed in בעל בעמיו *Ba'al Be'amaw*. The tensions between the demands of the social group and the individual are not satisfactorily resolved. But we may still put the question as to whether it is merely the chance encounter which precipitates conflict and disaster, or whether there is not some quality inherent in the nature of the hero that has not made this conflict inevitable. If the latter is the case, then the particular plot and its erotic dress are rather the working out of a great quality that is pre-existent. The Eros may be the manifest subject matter, but the substratum is the tension between a given social context and a particular sort of character, the Burla hero. Thus we may distinguish between the manifest and the real subject through an analysis of these stories.

* * *

Burla's work, deals with material not intimately familiar to the contemporary Hebrew reader. For various complex reasons, the Islamic world and the Jewish roots within that world have only quite recently been made the material of modern narrative prose. But in Burla's stories, we get a glimpse of Jewish-Muslim relations in the Middle East and something of the twentieth century context with the emergence of Zionism. But Burla does not relate exclusively of Jewish contacts. בלי כוכב *Beli Kokhav* (Luckless, 1920) is a story of internicine Arab rivalry, of an ancient feud between tribes.[4] The narrator within the story is Abd, a Bedouin soldier serving in the Turkish army. He relates that he had been adopted by the Hafani tribe, but that although he had been protected and cared for by the tribe, he never felt completely an equal but rather, as his name would suggest, an inferior (*abd* "slave"). As with all Burla's stories there is a conflict, and again as usual, that conflict is expressed in terms of a prohibited love. Abd loves Sheikh Farhan's daughter, which, for an inferior, not a genuine, fully accepted member of the tribe, is impermissible. Abd is driven to a frenzied search for his mysterious origins, perhaps brought on by the external rejection, and he discovers that he is of the Katifi tribe. These Katifi are very estimable in tradition. They had once sheltered the Prophet Muhamad, who had pronounced, 'The Katifi will never pass away from the earth! Any tribe which fights the Katifi intending to wipe it out—the curse of the Prophet be on

---

[4] A subject also treated from within the Arab perspective by the Hebrew writer Yitzhak Shami in נקמת האבות *Niqmath Ha'avoth* (Tel Aviv, 1928).

it! That tribe will disappear from the earth'. So Abd is a grudgingly protected individual, although, as he discovers, these Hafani have killed his family. His second conflict is whether he should take revenge. After all, the Hafani have, in a sense, saved his life, and, in any case, they are his beloved's own family. In order to grasp the depth of the conflict, we have to appreciate the sense of honour amongst Bedouin and their bounden duty to exact revenge in any circumstances. His beloved Nehora adopts a different attitude, and, in this context, a revolutionary one: 'Resentment and hatred belonged to our ancestors. We have love and peace, with Allah's will'. So Nehora here expresses what Daud, what Akaviah, what Rahamu and what Gideon have expressed within the framework of other novels: the assertion of individual instinct over the norms of the community. Two values are here brought into opposition. And it is interesting that in spite of the disparity of context, the dénouement is similar. The couple opt to persist in their love. They marry and go to live in Beirut. But again, it seems that their predetermined Kismet (Fate), their Star, will not move away. Firstly, he, Abd, falls into a depression, missing his homeland in the south. And then, Nehora's family, like Nemesis, eventually tracks them down and takes its revenge by slaughtering Nehora and the children. Abd lives to tell the story to the primary narrator, a Jew acting as interpreter in the Sinai desert during the Great War. But that Fate has taken its normal course.

Through this process of analysis of the Burla story, stripping the plots down to their skeletal elements, we can arrive at certain conclusions. The central conflict analysed is not one that stems from the specifically modern situation. It does not reflect the European-style Enlightenment, i.e. the tendency to subject tradition to scientific examination, nor the existential predicament producing alienation from the environment. The conflict and the rebellion are those known to generations past, within the religious tradition, the social tradition, and amongst the Oriental communities. The predicament is that of instinct as opposed to the social norm, either Jewish or Arab. Religiously, we do find a strain of questioning amongst the heroes of the tales. Indeed, there would have to be, to permit such taboo associations as are here proposed. But the questioning is not particularly of the type that we associate with the secularisation process in modern Hebrew literature, or with the post-

Enlightenment, culturally assimilating Jew of the 'West'. it is rather a 'universal', sometimes mystical investigation of a specific 'tribal' loyalty. The 'wise man' when called in for counsel by the troubled protagonist, often involves a truth beyond than the specific loyalty. God, as Akaviah has said, has His sphere, and man his. It is trivialising to expect God to be personally provident. And if this line of thought is accepted, then certain consequences are drawn for human and social behaviour. If God is an abstract source of truth, He is unlikely to insist on parochial attachments. People are not to be divided into Jew, Muslim and Christian; they all partake of the qualities of mankind. In נפתולי אדם *Naftuley adam*, we have one of the most interesting attempts to offer consolation to the stricken hero. Rahamu, in his raving, frustrated blindness, turns away from his God. How could He countenance such a terrible fate for one of his creatures? (Although Rahamu has provided a possible answer by saying that as his eyes, his source of attractiveness, and his own lust, moved him along his path, so they are now removed.) But the wise man who acts as his counsellor, Sheikh Abdul Karim al-Tunisi, teaches Rahamu not to blame God. God is not like man—vengeful or spiteful. It is not He who has blinded Rahamu and caused him to suffer. Rahamu is taught to accept truth uncomplainingly. Rahamu learns too from the sufferings of his father who has gone through so much hitherto unheeded by his son. After his father's death, he returns to synagogue and resolves to discover 'what my life really meant'. And he is resolved too to become the sole gauge of good and evil, i.e. not to accept secondhand doctrines, but to establish them for himself. This enables him to put up with situations, even things more terrible than before, such as the death of his beloved Shafikah, driven to suicide by the abuse of her relatives. The doctrine that he then propounds is redolent of Sufism—with the loss of everything, the true self can be found: 'Yet only then, when I had lost all—the light of my eyes, all hope of love and faith—only then did I find the one thing of value: I found myself'. In his view at least, he had now found the true God by breaking free of the chains of imaginary gods. He can now do what he thinks he ought to do. And this is what makes him into the character we meet at the beginning of the story—charming, open, self-accepting. He is perhaps somewhat lax in external observance, but he is a person who has come to terms with himself and his world.

* * *

This, then, is the Burla hero. He is not particularly of our modern times, nor specifically of the context familiar to the contemporary reader. The story is told essentially in terms of morality; even if those terms do not seem to apply, appeal is made to that court. It is plotted in traditional manner, with a beginning, a middle and an end. It revolves around a single person (hero, adventurer of the picaresque), whose psychology is grasped whole and simple, and to whom things happen in sequence. The question that his hero poses too is one of good and evil the former to be rewarded and the latter to be punished. The problem remaining is the nature of that morality. Is the traditional group loyalty adequate to cover the events as they unfold? Is the teaching and behaviour pattern as relayed by the group necessarily and universally unimpeachable? The hero of these stories learns to think otherwise, not as a result of abstract speculation, but from his own life experience. Akaviah wants to save Diamante, beloved replica of Anaheit. If wrong is done to her, and it is presumed to be done or at least permitted by God, then God must be at fault. So the hero is in conflict with the conventional morality and the conventional religion as taught to him by his teachers and as propagated by his group. Diamante's fortune is bound up with his own, and she should not be allowed to suffer: "I would correct your star ... I would save you and save myself ... that I should effect this great reparation'.

The fact that Akaviah can rail against Fate, and then tell God that as a consequence he is leaving Him, implies a primary assumption of His existence and His providence. The taught morality is assumed so that it might be challenged. Once the teaching of the Sheikh in נפתולי אדם *Naftuley adam* becomes operative, not only can the question no longer be answered, it cannot even be asked. If God be confined to His sphere and allowed no involvement in man's affairs, then the problem must be viewed quite differently. Man's destiny becomes the sole concern of man. It is no longer the intended product of external manipulation, but rather the necessary consequence of man's own free action. This is how Rahamu comes to a self-acceptance. As long as he accepted his lot as imposed, he had to protest at the injustice. Even if he had done wrong, surely the evil could not have been so great as to warrant such terrible retribution or any sort of external imposition. So he becomes a self-authenticating entity. This is his freedom, as he sees it.

I have tried here to delineate the nature of Burla's writing—the sort of tale told, the ethical assumptions, the movement of the plot, the typology of the argument and the character of the central figures. It can be placed historically and intellectually (except for some incidental trappings realting to contemporary events) in the context of the mediaeval tale. The oriental colour augments that impression, e.g. the liberal use of Arabic or Ladino vocables to convey the speech and thought patterns of the protagonists. There is no stylistic or linguistic experimentation. And the type of conflict that we have dwelt on so much, for all its bitterness and vivid reality, belongs to the pre-modern world. So does the plotting, the logical sequence, the build-up, the climax and the disappointment of the moral. Above all, character is grasped in the pre-modern sense—not fragmented, not represented by a stream of consciousness, not recognised as essentially problematic. It is true that some individuals in the stories (Daud in אשתו השנואה *Ishtho Hasenuah* for example) do not recognise their own nature, and so act against it. But the basic nature is taken as unchangeable, even when it is not recognised for what it is. The 'evil inclination', the driving libido, is the implied root of the character, motivating him unconsciously. The author realises that the character may be either distracted by his own subjectivity or inefficiently sophisticated to recognise what is happening. Nevertheless, the character is not only grasped whole, but there is an assumption that there exists a graspable nature within him, even if this goes beyond the character's own articulated frame of reference. The range of possibilities is bifurcated, i.e. there are two, not an infinite number, nor an irresolute splinter. What we have is basically a naive grasp of man's psychology within the traditional Hebrew tale.

AMALIA KAHANA-CARMON AND THE PLOT OF THE UNSPOKEN

The Israeli prose writer Amalia Kahana-Carmon has produced a sort of story and novel generally out of step with the mainstream of Israeli literature. Her output in hard covers is thus far limited to a volume of short stories בכפיפה אחת *Bikhefifah Ahath* (1966) a novel וירח בעמק אילון *We Yareah Be' Emeq 'Ayalon* (1971) and a 'triptych', שדות מגנטיים *Sadoth Magnetiyim* (1977). But even with her first appearance in print, a different voice was recognised. The critic Grodzenski, for example, recalling his immediate impressions of the story החמה נסתלקה *Ha-hamah Nistalquh*, published in 1956, says; 'The picture is not a panorama, but a single landscape, something on its own. The intention is a fragment of reality'.[1] Since that time, there has been discussion of the worth of this prose, but little doubt expressed about its unusual character within the Israeli context.

Israeli fiction writing of the post-State period commonly reflected the broader political reality. With the emergence of independence, the Hebrew writer in Palestine was becoming a self-aware Israeli, inevitably forging the linguistic and literary tools to achieve expression of this new fact. A state at war needs confirmation of its heroism and a portrait of its heroes. Israel received this most popularly in the novels (as well as in the plays and stories) of Moshe Shamir. The conscience of that society in action, of the individual as pressurised by the emergent social group, was expressed by S. Yizhar. Social institutions of the society were characterised by writers of the generations such as H. Bartov (born 1926) and N. Shaham (born 1925). And when at a later stage, the Israeli writer felt himself free to cast doubt on accepted values, whether articulated or implicit, this attack was still conducted within the framework of the larger society where the stories' characters operated and in which the situation was created. Even novelists of an earlier generation such as H. Hazaz were constantly commenting on the new social environment as the primary

---

[1] *Davar* 30.7.71.

concern of the story. S. Y. Agnon, that ironic commentator on the Jewish scene, drew individual character in a symbolic mode but still cast an eye on the society at large. When the time came for the writer to express total disenchantment with that society to the extent of registering his indifference to it or alienation from it, this took the form of a search for supranational values and metaphysical concern, as in the work of P. Sadeh (born 1929).

Such examples could be multiplied. I have invoked a broader context to indicate the special sort of prose that Kahana-Carmon was to introduce to the Israeli literary scene. Elsewhere, I have described her work as 'intensely concerned with the analysis of interpersonal relationships and their refraction on a particular individual', and said further that she 'has subjected the individual consciousness, particularly that of the female, to the sort of analysis that we are familiar with in Virginia Woolf'.[2] This is not to say that the cast of mind portrayed is close to that of Woolf's characters, or that such is the case for the movement of the story. But what does recall a certain strand of the English narrative tradition is this 'intense concern' with the psychical movement of the individual. More precisely, in relation to the memory of a previous state or condition, as affected by others, or as that individual relates to others. She portrays an almost mystical sense of union with the other (as so often, a seemingly arbitrary selection of a figure in the narrative), not as it exists objectively, or as perceived by this other, but as recorded by the subjective mind. Naturally, this exclusive subjectivity leads to disappointment. In this sense, Kahana-Carmon's writing is romantic. The contrast is offered between the ideal and the actual, even if both these states are entirely products of the troubled consciousness. The writing tries to portray very precisely and intensively the sense of loss, that 'small death' (as she once described it) that constantly recurs, not only for the adult recalling a more vivid childhood, but also for the child meeting a blunt reaction. There is an inevitable frustration becoming poignant sadness.

The instrument for the achievement of this effect is her language. The unusual quality of the author's language saves

[2] See Yudkin, *op. cit.*, pp. 171-2.

her stories from what would otherwise be eccentricity or sentimentality. So precarious is the link that she establishes with external reality (i.e. that sense of things not created by the moving mind in the story) that extra demands are made on the creative power of the word. The word has to conjure up its own credibility, because the view of the subject is not often confirmed by other participants in the story or by the events described. As the author, in order to achieve such credibility, must build a unique universe, her created language must depart from the norm. These linguistic deviations have been attacked. Literary Hebrew is not yet crystallised to the extent that it can easily absorb irregularity. We are immediately aware in a Kahana-Carmon story that not only does her language not correspond closely with the prevalent vernacular, but that it sometimes significantly departs too from the dominant convention in literature. These occasional departures permeate the whole and create a different tone. And this tone becomes the reality. Her language is poetic prose. By this, I mean that it moves, thus moving us, into another sphere. To demonstrate this explicitly and exhaustively is difficult, both because I am using the medium of another language in our description, and because I cannot demonstrate these points statistically. But here are some peculiarities.

The language of her dialogue does not generally shift into another register. Normally, a writer has one sort of language for the description of events and his own perceptions, and a different one for the record of speech. This latter is based on a 'tape recorder' model, i.e. it tries to imitate actual tone of voice and idiom. The difference in function between the two modes would, in the majority of cases, normally demand a different register. Such a difference would be most accentuated when the author's narrative language is rich, multilayered, cultured, literary and subtle, and when the characters portrayed are linguistically limited (e.g. children). Speech, in any case, does not deploy its full potential range, but such a situation would highlight the contrast. S. Yizhar's work illustrates this point, where the movement from authorial description to representation of speech, is sharp. In Kahana-Carmon's stories, this happens rarely (although there are exceptions). The language of speech, as represented in the mouths of the characters, is generally literary, high, and of a character similar to the narrative language throughout.

Although this language, as noted, is literary, it is not always grammatised in the traditional manner. Literary Hebrew usage has certain conventions, and, although liberal and flexible in some ways, e.g. in word order, it does nevertheless impose bounds on expression. A subject normally requires a verb and an object. This grammatical regularity is sometimes absent in the language of Kahana-Carmon. There are incomplete sentences which conclude in a row of dots. The relative pronoun is occasionally left out where you might otherwise expect it. Here, Mrs Talmor in וירח בעמק אילון *We-Yareah Be'emeq Ayalon*, sadly reflects on her own situation, in a sentence which has been criticised, 'When I see older couples, the children have grown up, she thought, to me they are like remains on a battlefield'. We would normally expect a relative pronoun or ablative absolute (in the Latin structure) to be inserted before 'the children'. And yet the effect is deliberately contrived. This lack of smoothness is to the author's purpose.

There are unusual forms of the Hebrew language, and words used in what is now an unusual sense. The appearance of אפס *efes* as 'but', for example, can have nothing but an archaising effect. This is a Biblical usage, common in Hebrew poetry through the ages, and, in prose, reinstated by writers of the 'Enlightenment'. It has, however, been generally dropped by narrative writers in the twentieth century. The same is true of the phenomenon known variously as the 'waw consecutive' or 'waw conversive', apparently shifting the tense from perfect to imperfect and vice versa. There are still traces of this in the Hebrew prose of the early part of the century. But, in the contemporary context, it is archaic and archaising, poetic. The author uses it even within such as prosaic sentence as (lit.); 'He lifted up his legs and went'.

A phenomenon closely linked to וישא את רגליו וילך the point about literary language, but not identical with it is the author's tendency to offer lists of objects in place of sentences. In the introduction to the story החמה נסתלקה *Hahamah Nistalqah*, for example, after opening with; 'I remember the palace', she then presents the reader with thirty lines of names of objects. The purpose of this 'catalogue' is presumably to recreate the desired atmosphere in a very concrete and specific way, reminiscent of Robbe-Grillet's attempted neutrality in the 'nouveau roman'. But here, every part of the description does hold an emotional charge; it is not only to represent the garden of the palace as accurately as possible, but also to suggest a character that is dying. The subject of the story is the passing of that old world in England, and we hear that the 'palace' is to be sold off. Its inhabitants too are physically dying: 'There will come a time when there won't be a trace of the aristocracy left in England'.

The author's use of metaphor sometimes gives the description its specific character. It has long been said that metaphor is the poet's most particular mode.[3] Kahana-Carmon seeks to achieve this specificity, not through use of traditional Hebrew phraseology, nor even through the recasting of the traditional mould. In the story האור הלבן *Hoar halavan*, she tries to convey the character of the Swiss village where she, the narrator, is staying with her husband Alex: 'The town pushed us up together like an ant heap, was made of a wall of one cast, its edges jagged and its towers sharpened pencils'. The atmosphere sought is one of peculiarity and isolation that may highlight her own inner sadness.

These special linguistic devices converge to create a narrative voice which remains separate from the world familiar to most of us. The tone of the author gathers strength from the implied contrast with something else, or with a memory. This memory is undoubtedly romantic. It is relieved of sentimentality by the reader's sense that he is not being presented with what pretends to be an objective portrait of a situation. When the author, in the story אני צמא למימייך ירושלים *Ani tzame lmemayikh Yerushalayim* (also reproduced in her novel as a flashback memory) writes, 'You were at kindergarten. You were a school pupil. You were at high school. Now you are a student at the Hebrew University. A new period. Jerusalem. City of spices. I am soaked here in a constant state of light dizziness', we might normally consider this somewhat absurd. But this elevated romanticising of the past, or of that other, is the very fabric of the author's vision. The extreme roseate tinge proffered to her sense of the inescapably lost is the linguistic character that Kahana-Carmon puts on to vitalise her sense of things. We know that we are not necessarily expected to see Jerusalem as she suggests in the passage. But we do know that we are getting a glimpse of her vision at second remove.

* * *

---

[3] Aristotle, *Poetics* 22.

So much discussion has been devoted to the nature of Kahana-Carmon's language because it is clearly by the specific use of her own language that she achieves the desired effect. Her object is to illustrate the history of a personality—that is, how it changes, how it is affected. We learn about this personality however, not only through the words themselves, but also through the gaps between the words. As G. Shaked writes in his discussion of the private world that emerges in her writing, 'The ellipses between the pictures are more important than the pictures themselves'.[4] The reader is more aware of the intended emotional impact of a story or incident or meeting than of the precise succession of events. In the story בכפיפה אחת *Bikhefifah ahath*, we are introduced to a primary theme of the author's: the inexplicable and intense attraction on the part of the principal character towards another person. Here it is experienced by a male character. The source of the attraction is Bruno, who is first introduced with a gnomic utterance. Then, when invited to join them in listening to the radio, this chief character says, 'The instrument was of Bruno's making and with that he conquered me. But even without the radio I would have thought of him a lot'. This translation does not capture the ethereal quality of the original, but we still perceive that we are presented with a puzzle. No explanation is offered as a reason for the attraction, nor is the question raised. We are presented with the fact. We only know that 'In my eyes he was inexplicable and different. He was like a house without windows'. A window grants the spectator access to view, and also some insight as to the house's arrangement. But Bruno does not possess this advantage, and so must remain a mystery. This mystery has an analogue at the story's conclusion, when a conversation takes place between the narrator and his hero. A screw top falls to the ground, and when he stoops to pick it up, he notices two shadows cast although there is only one light bulb. Bruno tries to solve the puzzle and explain the mystery. But when he discovers that the explanation is not convincing, he resigns himself to failure; 'If that's the case I don't know then. I'm not a good teacher. Go to sleep now'. This is the end; we are left with two mysteries. The duplicate shadow from the

---

[4] גל חדש בספורת העברית *Gal Hadash Ba Siporeth Ha 'Ivrith* (Tel Aviv, 1970) p. 171.

light bulb suggests a reverberation beyond the immediate cause. This, too, is the case with Bruno.

Here is the nub of the difficulty in Kahana-Carmon's writings. In her description of the individual psyche, the author is reconciled to the non-rational; effect is not matched by cause. This phenomenon is suggested by the verbal texture. Thus, the gap can be as suggestive as the word. Time sequence may be irregular. Memory can intervene in present activity. Attraction is mysterious and evanescent. Personality undergoes strange shifts; the gear changes abruptly. Because we are in a strange world, the language undergoes this distancing process. We may not understand what is going on, but we might experience part of it. That is how the author's success might be measured.

* * *

Memory, or memory reconstructed, obtrudes itself on the present. The makeup of the personality is created by contrasts. Again, we are not necessarily faced with two alternative realities; one might be a conjured possibility of the mind. In the story ברחוב *Barhov*, a man and woman, whose paths had not crossed for thirteen years, meet up again twice in quick succession. In the interim period, they had gone their separate ways. We saw in החמה נסתלקה *Hahamah Nistalqah* the death of an old world with the physical death of the Lord of the Manor. That story turns on a potential contrast. A new world is emerging, even if its only known characteristic is the absence of what is then described as disappearing. Here, in ברחוב *Barhov*, another contrast is drawn—what had been or what seemed to have been in the minds of the two protagonists, with what is now. Can the past be brought back, is the implied question. The two linger together; 'The accidental encounter seemed to be accidental no more'. Again in this story, communication is established between them on a level deeper than the words might suggest. She is angry with him, and the reason that she offers is that his father gave her a low mark for Nature Study at school. But when challenged, she admits that this is not the true reason. Something is happening in the story beyond the realm of the spoken. As the dialogue develops, we hear the recurrent Kahana-Carmon theme, as he says to her 'you were different from them all'. The past seems to be resurrected although this assumption is constantly questioned. 'What is left as it was, I mean left as it was?' he asks. But his conclusion is that 'in sum, there is nothing left but small moments of revelation'. And this is taken together with 'moments of revelation of hair falling out, and teeth, in my case'. Time's movement is inexorable and disastrous. The two must be taken together; he will still preserve the picture of 'another Joshua', a grand cavalier on a splendid stallion, with this other girl from his past. The story ends with 'And the whole world is in expectation of great deeds'.

Another story באר־שבע בירת הנגב *Beersheva Birath Hanegev* also builds on the dissonance between the fantasy of a person and his reality. In this case, there is a tragic reality because the object of the female narrator's fascination, Noah, is killed (the story is set in Beersheba during the War of Independence). Of Noah, she reflects, 'Why is he so anonymous, with the clothes hanging on him, his touching walk, as though a blind man were before you and you were shy to read his exposed features'. This is the inexplicable attraction. But how cope with the natural phenomenon of death? The story, at its end in fact, moves away from the confrontation; '"Beersheba", stresses the bartender, "Beersheba is the capital of the Negev"'. Again, a contrast, though here of a different sort; the contrast of escape into anti-climax. Both the particular world and individual within it are fragile. People are placed in a glass menagerie. But, of course, the glass may be broken.

Enough now has been said of Kahana-Carmon's writing to indicate something of the nature of the literature that she aims to produce. There is a basic emotional situation which is described, a point of view through which an account emerges. There is description but not explanation or ratiocination, however odd or arbitrary this account might appear to be. A reality is created, a specific reality for each story and novel, although much is common to all. We have seen a little of how the linguistic process creates this reality, how the reality becomes obsession, but is then contrasted with another reality. The narrative voice in the stories is pathetically fragile, glowingly hopeful, but also simultaneously regretful. The final dénouement of inevitable disappointment is anticipated together with the hope. As she writes in one story, התרוששות *Hithroshshuth*, 'I who pursue cannot reach what I am supposed to, the wave which has turned over inside me at the sight of the sea and stirred feelings of other seas'. There is never satisfaction—one thing recalls another. We saw how in ברחוב

Barhov, Joshua images another Joshua. Here, one sea stirs feelings for other seas.

The intense subjectivism of the stories has inevitably led to the label of Impressionism. Impressionism is that tendency where the artist as subject soaks up 'impressions' of the external world for record, without previously imposing on them a total vision or doctrine. The impressionist work resembles a mosaic (at least in theory), because the total is composed of fragments of a reality as reflected by the subject. The stories of Kahana-Carmon are intensely subjective, whether told from the point of view of adult or child, male or female, whether the account is first or third person. A well known story of hers נעימה ששון כותבת שירים *Ne'ima Sason Kotheveth Shirim* is, as it were, actually recounted by the child of that name herself, in her recall of a childhood passion and its related incidents, as though she were still a child. This is the impression of childhood. The author has often presented catalogues of objects to reify a situation. She can also do this through recollected dialogue and action. The child, obsessed with her teacher Yehezkel, seeks every opportunity to be with him, and dedicates to him a poem called 'My Teacher', which is hung up on the classroom wall. Again, she speaks to him as someone of 'a special kind', what is it that bothers her? Here, the narrator adopts a metaphor which recurs regularly with Kahana-Carmon, 'The animal cub that I have borne on my heart for many days, its nails in my flesh yearning to scratch, pulling at the reins'. The animal is the name of the obsession. Something uncontrollable and wild is disturbing from within. The only possible release is articulated, ironically, by the child; 'Everyone senses the wonder within his own heart. But I, when I grow up, God willing, I'll know how to put down in writing all wonders. I must. Otherwise my life is not living'. So here is the story.

In another story ממראות הבית עם מדרגות המסוידות תכלת *Mimaroth habayith 'im madregoth hamsuyadoth tkheleth*, the narrator (Tirzah) actually speaks of herself as having one foot in one reality, and the other in a second. The two merge in a series of mutually intrusive impressions. But here, she wants things to remain as they have been. To her regret, Anoch, her previous obsession, has changed, so that the situation is not as it was. But the faithful companion Isaachar is now standing stroking her hair: 'I wanted that moment to continue and not go away'. The central metaphor (taken from the title) is the blue steps. If you mount the steps you'll be snatched up: 'Nothing will be as it was'. Then you change, and what you have had becomes just a memory.

The trouble is that people will not heed the lesson: 'Adults enter of their own free will into complex situations. In normal times, there is no one like me who so fears confrontations'. (זכיה מן ההפקר *Zkhiyah min hahefqer*). This story, about a girl who comes to England and tries to record her impressions of the country, tells both literally and metaphorically of danger. She goes to the fair, even to the Wall of Death. But, we learn, adults do not heed danger. They mount the blue steps. That is what seems to happen in Kahana-Carmon's stories. The disaster has already occurred, and can now only be recorded.

* * *

Awareness of the other's specialness inhabits the Kahana-Carmon protagonists when they meet each other. In the story פעמון הזכוכית *Pa'amon hazkhukhith*, Abigail tells the narrator, on first acquaintance, 'There is something special about you'. Then the story begins, and the title comes into force: 'A sort of glass bell was placed over the two of us, separating us off from the rest'. Each one is special to the other, so together they comprise a quintessential unit, isolated as an island within the large London scene. Not only does the particularisation here contribute to the composition of the story, but there is an explicit recognition of this fact: 'Everything belongs to the matter. The headlines written out in white chalk on the black surface, the newspaper saleslady, her piercing throat wrapped in a check scarf, the little man leaning with cheap elegance against the street post, his hat at an angle'. The detail is the picture. And Abigail articulates his lack—the Virginia Woolf connection. He does not have 'a room of his own', an announcement which he accepts as a verdict on himself, which he accepts too with equanimity. The 'room of one's own' is here the authentic expression of personality; Woolf's aspiration out of frustration becomes a metaphor for the appropriate life style of the individual. His individuality has been recognised. Now he must find the means sufficient for its fulfillment.

This story is so typical of Kahana-Carmon. The setting, the meeting, the sudden attraction, the recognition of affinity, and then the loss. Because, very soon after the connection is made, it is cut off for no apparent reason. She visits him at his office, and asks him a pedestrian question. Then 'It seemed that she was also embarrassed. As though we both expected a miracle which did not recur'. The whole relationship has reverted to the prosaic quality of the everyday; 'Gone is the wonderful feeling of specialness. No longer unique in quality. And the glass bell, what will be with the glass bell?' And he recognises that he has not got a room of his own. They do meet again, perhaps with a view to repairing the damage. But 'when the glass bell is broken, there is no hope for it, I know. Abigail will be just a strange girl whom I had met by chance on an ordinary day, on a bench in a public park'.

The author does seem to recognise the oddness of the incident described. It seems to be so commonplace. Towards the end of this short story, she comments on it, 'In any case, here is a small story of an incident, confused as it is. How people vainly reach out their hands to each other...'. She then compares the event to the leaf from Mount Ararat in the Biblical story of the Flood, 'an embalmed sprout that withered and died'. How easily can something come to an end if it is not allowed to flourish in its natural environment! Thus she illustrates the unpredictable fragility of the rare moment, a sudden meeting's lightning flash which quickly darkens again. And then, as in so many of her stories, anti-climax. A drab street scene, with buskers singing 'The Duke of York': '... When they were only half way up, they were also half way down'. This twilight existence is the norm which has now been re-entered.

* * *

Youth contrasted with middle age, boundless hope with acceptance of grey reality, is the theme of Kahana-Carmon's novel וירח בעמק אילון *Weyareah Be'emeq Ayalon*. The title is taken from Joshua 10:12, where God halts the sun and moon in their tracks in order to enable the Hebrew leader Joshua to achieve his victory over the Amorites. This, as suggested by the comment that follows in the Biblical book, was a one-time event never to be repeated. In the novel here, we see the middle-aged Mrs Talmor going through a romantic experience with Philip, the foreign visitor to Israel. But we also see her as Noah, the young student in Jerusalem, in the extract that was published earlier as a separate story, אני צמא למימייך ורושלים *Ani tzame lmemayikh Yerushalayim*. Her husband, Asher, has been the fanatical, politically motivated young man of that section, so typically, a source of limitless fascination. But now Asher is the successful businessman, bored with her neuroticism, and happy to leave her in the charge of the visiting expert. Mrs Talmor has not ceased to be the romantic Noah, but now she has 'to learn a new language'. Because, with time, things change. As Rotman, the legal adviser says; 'In every married woman something is broken'. Those student times serve as the necessary contrast. Then 'the squirming beast in my breast rested as though sated to loss of senses'. She had been obsessed with Asher, and he with her.

But this is not the total picture: 'We so want to believe that we are as we are in our fine moments'. The 'fine moments' represent the peaks from which mortals have to make their descent to the lowlands. Mrs Talmor's sickness is her dis-satisfaction, in the words of Proverbs, 'the leech with daughters give give', always asking for more. As she iterates regularly; 'The desire always to be at the top, never to stop at less'. Philip too, disturbed, asks how she can manage 'without the technique of the weak. She has not learned the efficient technique of the mediocre'. The present conflict between Asher and Noah is of a different order. For Asher, Noah is useless, 'a woman who doesn't raise a finger, someone without whom the world could carry on without noticing the difference'. For Noah (now the mature Mrs Talmor), Asher lacks the imaginative capacity to share her world, and so he is contemptuous and rejects it. People, in order to cope, reject what they cannot understand. Noah recognises her own apparent irrationality. Why can she not be happy with all her abundance of good fortune? After all, life itself is 'something that comes as a gift'. And as for Philip, his fascination is utterly mysterious. He is 'the messenger from the regions of brightness', from another realm, bearing the transforming message. On the other hand, she must come to terms with the brutal fact; 'We will never go up together to the top of the Shalom tower'. We have already encountered the image of 'height' as epitomising aspiration. Now, even Tel-Aviv's tallest building is beyond the heroine's capacity. In a later conversation with a student friend, the essence of the disillusion is summarised. Those student days still live in the present as an indication of negative possibility: 'Everything that we thought we should live for we must now do without'. Those radiant visions are to be buried. The dream is different from the reality. A student friend of hers, Bruriah, acts as a sort of parallel to Mrs Talmor's own situation. She is constantly 'being prepared for something which should occur but which never does'. These are the romantic types, offering unbridled, frustrating and elusive possibility. This is Mrs Talmor's story, incomplete as indicated at the end of the novel, ultimately concerned, on the human level, with hope, fulfillment, disappointment and reconciliation, and, from the literary point of view, with the word. As said in an imaginary interview conducted by a writer, there is 'again an encounter with words'. Nothing else, no other reality.

Much of the novel tries, with linguistic virtuosity, to capture the specific sense of place—Tel Aviv, Jerusalem, Eilat and Israel generally. In *Hithroshshuth*, there is an intense evocation of Tel-Aviv on the part of the girl seeking out her lover. There is a memory of the past, just as it seems that the condition of the city recalls a certain (if necessarily brief) history. But in the recollection of that past, that inevitable end was presaged in the lived experience: 'But we exchanged words carefully. We know that these are only the last stirrings of what has clearly been condemned to extinction'. Relationships raise questions as does the town: 'Tel-Aviv is a town about which "who is she really" people ask themselves, even when they've lived there all their lives'. The story is a sad one, because it suggests that, now, only the past remains. As for the indexer (such is her profession), she is fascinated by lists of items and information. And when she works, 'the heritage of the past swings back and forth, and we know neither its meaning nor its object'. There remains still the question of, for example, why she came to meet him. But that remains a mystery. As the story ends, it is 'always preparation. For what, I do not know. Only preparation'.

When the author abandons the specificity of invocation, there exists the danger of evaporation, of a too hollow generality. And the repeated yearnings for the other time/other place, can be felt as mechanical. The sense of the title of the story, לב הקיץ לב האור *Lev haqayitz lev haor* suggests this. The one who expresses these longings here is the narrator's mother who, contrasted with the practical father, is not rooted in everyday reality, '... She has no contact with people'. She, too, is the one captured by the now well-established obsessive fascination, with Dr Bruchin. As usual, there is no successful resolution.

* * *

Paradoxically, although a writer's trade is words, and although Kahana-Carmon, through the imagined dialogue described above, has limited the potential confrontation of the writer to the word itself, we still note that non-verbal communication is the key factor in the interrelationship of the figures described. What the author does is to offer herself, recreated at various ages or in various guises. In a story מושכלות ראשונים *Muskaloth rishonim*, a man who started writing at a fairly advanced stage in his life, presents his theory or writing and his own credo. He divides writers into two sorts. The first type, the classical writer, imposes order on events. The second type imposes himself on the events which then take on his colour. The protagonist attaches himself to the second company. He, the writer, is the only thing genuinely present in the work, however fragile or indefinable that 'he' might be. When he offers his list of what his sort of writer might try to do, the first thing relates to the world—the atmosphere of place, time etc. and the second to the individual's relationship to these things. But it is clear that the first receives its character entirely from the second. He goes on to say that he approaches everything very personally and individually, although that describing voice would then become part of the object and its authentic nature. It is at this point that the picture, previously divided into its separate components, or, parochial in its nature, not belonging to anything but itself, becomes something larger and greater.

From where the author herself has suggested some sort of *ars poetica*, or more modestly expressed, a defined literary directive for a particular sort of writing, we too might try to observe her general direction. We do not have to confuse the author with the characters created or with the active narrator, but it does happen that these descriptions of a type of literary activity correspond closely with Kahana-Carmon's own writings. I have examined her carefully chosen language through which she individuates her world. I have also noted that that described world is seen from one severely confined point of view. I have observed the intense subjectivity of the descriptions. I have observed too, the key moment (whether explicit or implicit) in the stories, the 'peak', the happening, which is the meeting of two figures, the intense preoccupation with this figure or with the moment of the meeting, the attempt to recover that sense (the peak), and the disappointment in the wake of inevitable failure. this happening involves a communication, but the communication is mysterious and non-verbalised. In גלויות מצויירות *Gluyoth metzuyaroth*, a lady passenger travelling with her child on a ship, notices a lone man and becomes pre-occupied with him. We are not told that she is specially lonely or that he is particularly handsome. In fact, as in her writing generally, very little physical description of persons is given. But he is introduced by the narrative voice in quasi-religious tones. Whilst sitting on the deck, she sees him next to her. It is 'he and not another'—the words used in traditional Jewish literature to describe the direct intervention of God, stressing that there is no messenger acting for him. And indeed, this passenger, a vet, does act as a sort of God when the child is sick, assisting in the healing process. The attraction is mysterious, and when she seeks to articulate something of her feeling for him, she finds that she does not succeed. She gets confused; 'I wanted to tell you something else. But it seems that I'm talking and getting mixed up. I think that you don't understand me'. His triumphant agreement follows, 'not at all'. Although she apparently is nevertheless convinced that deep down he does understand her, the reader is free to believe otherwise. Her communication has not been passed on verbally. Perhaps it has only taken place in her own mind. We do not know his mental processes. We only know that in the plot development she tries to persuade him not to leave the boat for his own destination. Or, at any rate, that they should stay together. He refuses.

Such odd attractions do not conclude satisfactorily. In the story אם נא מצאתי חן *Im na matzathi hen*, the commercial correspondence teacher becomes totally wrapped up with a male pupil, religious and gauche. His amazement at her attempted expedition is transparent. The reader might ask why she is so attracted. This story, like the others, does not provide an answer, only a fascinating illustration.

In this chapter I shall take four examples to illustrate attempts at experimentation in the Israeli novel.

זכרון דברים *ZIKHRON DVARIM* (MEMORY OF THINGS, 1977) BY JACOB SHABTAI

We have previous evidence of Shabtai's narrative talents in his earlier collection of stories, הדוד פרץ ממריא *Hadod Peretz Mamri* (Uncle Percy Takes Off, 1972), a series of grotesque fables, mingling the far-fetched, the whimsical and the tragic. This novel follows the same direction in a manner most intense and single-minded. We attend the fortunes and reflections of three friends, Goldmann, Tzezar and Yisrael over the period of nine months, between (as the first paragraph indicates), the death of Goldmann's father and Goldmann's own suicide.

Rare indeed is the comic novel on the current Israeli literary scene, but especially rare is the type of comic novel that Shabtai has produced here. Making no concessions to the reader, the work consists of but one extended paragraph. This is a technique difficult for the reader to absorb, because he could not possibly read this very long book at one sitting, the assumption to which this technique appeals. A reader needs breaks, aids and directions, normally afforded by paragraph and chapter divisions. This is a kind of consciousness novel, but neither of one single stream nor emanating from but one reflector. The narrative darts constantly from one character to another, with their tales and their sub-tales, from their histories to their current activities, from their thoughts and preoccupations to their frenzied actions or impotent inaction, and through it all there is the gnawing sense of life's oddities and overall senselessness זכרון דברים *Zikhron Dvarim* is a tragic comic novel. It is told as a sort of swallowed sentence, more in the manner of Proust than of any Hebrew model.

All pervasive is the sense of the book's opening, with the throw-away mention of the two deaths. The novel is about death, telling of life to illustrate the point that the most intensely imagined vitality, expressed in eating, fornicating, learning or whatever, is only an irrelevant distraction. Goldmann's dictum is that 'life is nothing but a journey into death ... and more— that death is the essence of life fulfilling itself in it towards a final fulfillment like the chrysalis becoming a butterfly, which being so, everyone should get used to the acceptance of death, which never comes too early'. For all the preponderance of exuberant and extravagant fun, the novel is totally bleak. The only processes conveyed are the inevitability and ugliness of aging and degeneration, the transitory nature of personal attachment (no-one seems able to express genuinely felt love), and the incapacity of all human effort to rise above the action. Art, such as Yisrael's organ playing, is invoked, particularly at times of crisis (e.g. after Goldmann's death when Yisrael tries to strike out an independent direction), but that too fails.

Goldmann embodies the doctrine of intentional death. Yisrael and Tzezar are left to look on. Tzezar, about whom more is related in this book than any other character, is the one to observe the coincidence of the two deaths, and the nine months (paradoxically, the period required to create life) separating them. His own life is a catastrophe, a tide against which he swims frenetically, with his numerous affairs and frenzied pursuits, and changes of activity and interest. His son is dying of leukemia, but his angry reaction to this arbitrary illness induces only greater anti-life sentiment, as he forces his mistress Tehilla to undergo an abortion. He sees life only 'as a distressing and meaningless humiliation, or as a great puzzle from which one must take as much pleasure as possible'. In sober or regretful moments he labels this attitude 'gay suicide'.

Not that there are not many principles to be found embodied in the novel. Goldmann's father had been a Zionist and a Socialist, a man of sterling character. Uncle Lazar had been a Communist, had fought in the Civil War in Spain, had gone off to the Soviet Union in pursuance of his ideology, and there had been exiled. After he had long been thought dead, he returned to Israel where be brought back the doctrine that there is no one single path to salvation. Ideals did once exist, though they seem now to have lost their validity. Experience has obliterated them. The heroes of the novel seem to be in search of a substitute guiding principle. Goldmann is prepared to accept the view expressed by one Manfred, 'that he does not believe in the absolute autonomy of man, that he creates his own self, that the world creates itself, and that the denial of God's existence can only be credited if one asserts the unfettered rule of instincts, without values'. One has seen what has happened in such a world without God. In principle, Goldmann adopts this view, i.e. that, as the death of God brings in its train a world empty of values, one should then recreate a God with content built on values. But apparently his effort to achieve a religious view-point ends in failure.

זכרון דברים *Zikhron Dvarim* is an amalgam of farce and tragedy, and through both, the figures try to perceive meaning. For Goldmann, this meaning is only death, the sole, genuine substratum of existence. The only purpose of life should be to try to look death squarely in the face; 'He tried to think of death and the dead with tranquillity and happiness, because, after all, death is the true substance of life, and he knew that there was nothing to fear in it'. This obsession with death does not mean that Goldmann does not seek the precise opposite, i.e. eternity, infinite extension of life. He would have liked to live for, say, another thousand years. But it is just the very impossibility of that attainment which renders its fascination. Death is ungraspable, terrifying, and thus, fascinating and seductive. Since death reigns supreme and inevitably must do so in the future, the only adequate response to death's dominance has to be submission to it. He would come to terms with the absolute dictator. What is the point of living a bit longer? Would another few years radically alter the situation? 'After all, everyone is going to die, and ten years more or less are not foing to make much difference one way or the other, as neither will boisterous living, but he would like to understand death and make a friend of it'. This is said of Goldmann (the novel is written entirely in the third person), whose individual solution sets the tone of the novel and then constitutes its dominant content.

This book can be read partly as a social critique. Here is Israeli society populated by the post-religious Jew, floundering in the enticing, open, uncharted sea of the world, excited but directionless. His capacity to swim in it and navigate it, is both limited and inevitably doomed. We then see life as a crazy game, the rider on the wall of death, which we, the readers, know must collapse. Goldmann, presumably the novel's chief hero, is the one most conscious of this. Tzezar is constantly trying to avoid the necessary conclusion, and so gets involved in his promising, but inevitably self-defeating and deflating, adventures. He is always disappointed with the development, but will still hold out hope for the next possibility. Yísrael is the most enigmatic of the three characters, living in the shadow of the other two, enjoying (if that could conceivably be said of him) Tzezar's hospitality, ineffectually attempting to render comfort to Goldmann, on the death of his father, to Tzezar, on the illness of his son and on his failed personal life. He is on the scene too after Goldmann's suicide. He tries to find comfort in his music, and then uproot, to change his life style and go to Jerusalem, where he might re-establish contact with his lost love. But he too fails in his attempt. The choice of options seems to move inexorably in an ever narrowing circle, and will eventually be closed off altogether. All these options may be in essence, imaginary too, because (for Goldmann) there is the decisive presence of the great sinister Master, undefeated and unvanquishable. The only way in which one can express genuine freedom of action, in Goldmann's view, is by anticipation of the inevitable event; 'Suicide is the fullest and total extraction of the freedom of choice that life offers, and it is also the freedom to renounce life itself, and to opt for what appears to be its opposite'. The paradox here is rooted in precisely this ambivalence; life, though infinitely desirable, nevertheless progresses through time into death. Death, so dreadful because unknown and thus inducing despair, must therefore be embraced. What Goldmann observes of the life around him is all doom laden. Life involves death—as with Tzezar's child, as with his own father, as with Tel-Aviv, the city which he recalls from his youth, which is now so changed. He is filled with hatred for the narrowness of everything around him. Far from newness holding out vitality and promise of a future, it heralds only the death of what went before: 'It (i.e. the recognition that it is he who is the stranger) could not modify the hatred that he felt for these new people and the feeling of helplessness and anger that swept over him in the face of this plague, changing and destroying everything, but, on the contrary, hatred and despair ate him up more bitterly than ever before and stimulated ever more his nostalgia and yearning for streets, neighbourhoods and landscapes that had been cut off forever, destroyed'.

Though this is not an easy book to read, it does eventually repay the effort. The fact that it is conveyed all on one level, in a monotone, does impose restraints, and force a justification of an eccentric technique. The novel has to rely then on the author's power to accumulate and transmit detail, both in character and in situation, which are rendered at times with considered vigour. The effect of the monotone can be hypnotic, as can the swing of the narrative in diverse directions, pointing different ways. But through all the crazy pastiche, flashes back and forward, tapestries of families and family circles, there does move a tragic sense, the memento mori most proudly borne by Goldmann, in the face of the self-indulgent, introspective lives of the strange but familiar figures who populate this novel.

* * *

המאהב *HAMEAHEV* (THE LOVER, 1977)
BY AVRAHAM B. YEHOSHUA

In recent years, Yehoshua, the prominent writer of a series of striking novellas, has commented on the difficulty of composing an Israeli novel. This genre is, after all, the product of a settled, multi-dimensional society reflecting on itself. But then, the author, presulably stimulated by his own challenge, produced that very thing, his first full-length novel.

In order to overcome the local difficulties, Yehoshua has selected a specific model, William Faulkner's *As I Lay Dying*, (1930), where the story is related, as it moves on, by each actor within. Thus המאהב *Hameahev* is narrated by six participants, including a single family of husband, wife and daughter, each one of whom sees the indubitably strange course of developments from his own viewpoint. Yehoshua has adopted this technique with considerable aplomb. The reader is held in a state of suspended expectation, as each contingent mystery slots into a further rung of the story, rather than meets a final resolution.

Adam, the Haifa garage-owner, observes his wife Assia's growing infatuation with Gabriel, the 'lover' of the story, with more than a tolerant eye. He, in fact, himself discovered Gabriel, who came to him as a client, an Israeli 'yored' (person who has left Israel) returned from his ten years' stay in Paris, as he thinks, temporarily, to pick up an inheritance. But Gabriel's return falls on the eve of the Yom Kippur War, his grand-mother (whose death he had expected) makes a temporary recovery, he enlists (under pressure from Adam) and disappears. Adam spares no effort in trying to trace him and to reconstruct what has happened. He seems to need the lover.

Adam's motivation is mysterious. The lover's disappearance is puzzling. Assia's infatuation is unexpected. Why is the dreamy daughter so troubled? Who is that man typing on the other side of the wadi who seems to to preoccupy her? And how does the young Arab lad, Naim, observe the goings on of Israeli, Jewish society? We have here tensions set up by a series of springs, arbitrary motivations interlocking and revolving around possible alterations of identity. Can Gabriel change his own essence by adopting the guise of the *Neturei Karta* sect in the course of the war? People assume that he is another, so perhaps he is.

Adam shares the lover with his wife, as established by his, and the novel's opening statement; 'And in the last war we lost a lover', which sets up both the puzzle and the expectation. As in Yehoshua's other stories, the narrative voice is 'confused' by the overwhelming impressions that flood him. The solution is elusive, because perhaps non-existent. We are presented with a gallery of figures in 'stunned' poses, who yet progress through a succession of charged events, always holding out the promise of climax. But there is a deliberate arbitrariness in the actions and decisions of the novel's characters. Is this an attempt to convey non-contingent decision, existence preceding essence? Things turn out unexpectedly. Vaduce, the ageing grandmother is traced from heavy incoherence to relieved awareness. An unlikely association is struck up between Naim and Duffy (the daughter). And Gabriel turns up when least anticipated, after months of search. This whole course of events is set in train by Gabriel's unsought migration to the battlefront. Gabriel is neither a fighter nor a patriot. He seems to be the unmoving moved, the effect rather than the cause. And he escapes his predicament by a shift from one unclearly delineated identity to another; one more vivid, but grotesquely inappropriate to his natural predilections. It is not that his convictions rebel against their imposition, but rather that his lack of conviction rejects definition.

In contrast to the changing silhouette of character, we have the force of external circumstances. The war is swift, violent and certain, sweeping these shadows of personalities with its power. For all the arbitrariness that should imply freedom, the figures in the novel, and particularly that of the lover himself, are in fact determined by such force. The plot is governed by this great war that no-one has expected or now understands. It is 'the certainty of a new reality overtaking us, that there is no retreat from it'. (Adam). This is the present, the point from the story takes off. But the past also comes across in the reflections and memories of the actors. We discover how this very 'quiet' marriage between Adam and Assia came about; a seemingly inappropriate combination of contrasting types—the controlled, unemotional, capable businessman not given to articulating his feelings and the vocal, hyperactive, intellectual though submissive woman. But again, these contrasting natures seem to complement each other and fulfil implied needs. The memory of their deaf son killed in a traffic accident, constantly moves in the background. In spite of their apparent cool, they are obsessed with common memories.

These monologues do not of themselves exhaust the speaker's feelings of thoughts. Yehoshua's language is usually sparse, spare and monotonous, insufficiently modulated to differentiate each character (though an exception must be noted in the remarkable portrait of Naim). The novel's strength lies in its movement, action and reaction; not in depicting self-awareness, but in the reflection of character in the plot. The author's range of vocabulary for the delineation of psychological states, though rigid and limited, can be compensated by the recognition of a monologue's limitations, and can allow unexpressed potentiality to emerge through the story. Implications, doubts and fears are the much greater shadows cast by the book's tight outlines. Even the novel's most explicit figure, Assia, constantly recounts her dreams, expressing what is inexpressible during conscious states. Adam does not know how to direct his control over people. He makes the action, finds a lover for his wife, 'sends' him to the war, searches for him unceasingly, raises Naim and drops him, intervenes in the life of the old lady, seduces his daughter's girlfriend, and yet does not understand his own motivation.

The 'lover', Gabriel Arditi, is finally traced by Adam towards the end of the novel, and one of the last monologues is Gabriel's own account releasing the tension of the unexplained mystery that has built up to such a crescendo. The pace of the search has quickened. Changes have been taking place, Adam becoming more frenetic, Naim maturing suddenly and with bitterness, Assia retreating into a sort of incommunicado frenzy of work, Duffy growing into an awareness of her sexuality, and of Naim. The empty vessel of Gabriel's personality is gradually filled with the contemporary reality of Israel in 1973. He is sent to the battlefront, but he can escape with members of the religious sect to which he is attracted because of 'their freedom. They don't actually belong to us. They came of their own volition, and they will go when they want. They owe nothing'.

There is no doubt that the specificity of the typology is to the author's advantage. That we have six named speakers rather than one anonymous narrator whose position shifts indeterminately, as in Yehoshua's other stories, adds bite to the work. In other of Yehoshua's stories, we are often uncertain who is recording the impression, and this can lead to an undisciplined exhibition of startling but uncontrolled effects. Here, there is an attempt to individuate character and situation within the unfolding plot.

If it is difficult to have various layers of narrative that emanate from the soil of social strata as background and fibre to that narrative, we do have in their place a multiple focus, where all reflect differently on the described rality. It is true that the language and characterisation of psychological states are somewhat limited and stereotyped, but the selection of such a narrative model has allowed the author to produce a work of genuine distinction.

* * *

חסות *HASUTH* (REFUGE, 1977) BY SAMMY MICHAEL

There are not so many Israeli novels that centre on the political crux of the local situation—the rivalry of Jew and Arab, the conflict for control of the Land. חסות *Hasuth*, the second novel [1] written by this writer of Baghdadi origin, who came to Israel as an adult shortly after the War of Independence, is precisely that. It tells a tale of revolutionaries, both Jew and Arab, and how they spend the first three days of the Yom Kippur War. It takes place principally at the Haifa home of Mardukh, whose biography is similar to the author's own, and of his wife Shula, a member of this revolutionary 'organisation', whose loyalties are divided. Mardukh willingly goes to fight, and Shula is asked by Arab members of the organisation to give refuge to a famous Arab revolutionary poet Fathi, on instructions from the leadership of the organisation. Shula is occasionally visited by

---

[1] The first is שוים ושוים יותר *Shawim Weshawim Yother* (Tel-Aviv, 1974).

Shoshana, a Jewish friend married to an Arab revolutionary called Fuad, by her own mother, also an ardent revolutionary, and by Turia, an elderly neighbour who quickly spots what is happening. And she also has the company of her retarded son, normally so dependent upon his father.

The complexity of human relationships is seen in the light both of biographical background, illuminated by constant flashbacks and fantasies, and of political arguments and situations. The question of the State's legitimacy is posed starkly and continuously. Evidently, even within the one group working towards a single end, loyalty is divided at the crunch. Mardukh goes to the war, and so inevitably fights to preserve the existence of Israel. But the organisation is working for the destruction of the State. Fathi preaches the Arab cause, is elated at the news of Arab successes, and yet he is taking refuge within Israel at the home of a fighter on the Israeli side. Shula's position is the most complex. She is a member of the organisation, and yet her husband is at the war, perhaps even dead or wounded. She is loyal to her husband, end yet she is housing a representative of the enemy he is fighting. The sexual situation parallels the military line-up. Fathi is alienating the affections of his friend's wife, and is aware of the proximity and vulnerability of a lovely woman (as she herself is aware of the attractive poet). So all are caught in a paradoxical trap, moving in opposite directions at the same time.

Hardly any character in this scenario lacks ambivalence. Fathi the poet preaches action, yet takes refuge. Mardukh works for a hostile organisation, then fights to nullify its aims. Shula's mother, we learn, deep down dislikes Arabs. Shula herself, in a moment of self discovery, decides to leave the organisation when she commits herself to her husband's cause in the war. She explains to her mother why Mardukh fights for Israel, in spite of being a declared revolutionary. It is a case of the 'refuge' of the title: 'Israel has offered him refuge. In the recesses of his heart, he felt that he owed a great debt to this land. He sees the mistakes, but he'll never forget that this was the only State which offered him a home'. Mardukh has been an active revolutionary in Iraq, but had then been rejected by that country. And he had been rejected even by the revolutionaries themselves as a Jew. Ambivalence applies in both directions. Fathi, who is such an anti-Israel ideologue, is, in the eyes of the Arabs of the refugee camps, so very Israeli in cast of mind, in approach, in his very success. After all, it is in Israel that he has thrived as a revolutionary poet: 'He is so great and famous that even Jews clap him when he tells them what bastards they are', says his friend Wasfi. Fathi too does not go all the way with some of the tactics adopted by the Group, and he dissociates himself from the murder of children. But in the opinion of a more committed revolutionary, Abla, this is a luxurious weakness. 'Revolutionary women despise inner turmoil, especially in men', ponders the poet. Shoshana, married to an Arab, is for this reason rejected by the Jews, but then she is not accepted by the Arabs either: 'Many doors were opened wide to her, but not hearts. At kindergarten, Amir (her son) was singled out from the rest of the children who saw in him a Jew, just as at the Jewish kindergarten, he had been regarded as an Arab'.

So this novel deals not only with a concrete situation set in a devastating war, casting the crystallised loyalties of the two races. It also raises the issue of identity within Israel (and beyond) in the twilight area of doubtful or dual allegiance. By setting the story at the point of most total conflict, this issue comes to a head. Not that any resolution is offered. The story breaks off after the third day of the war. Fathi, listening to Radio Cairo, believes that the Arabs have achieved total victory. Shula has rejected sexual adventure with him and made her own allegiance clear. All is in flux. We are not sure of Mardukh's fate. But we do see the dialectic in action, perhaps in a very obvious way. The crisis has brought to a head the need within each character for self-definition. Decisions have to be made, which, at least temporarily, remove the ambivalence. It seems that the two sides are fated to continue the dreadful, self-destructive struggle. As a member of the organisation says to Fuad, 'You've probably seen two dogs locked in copulation in the street, twisting, wailing, but unable to get away from each other's agony, pulling both ways. That's the Jews and Arabs in their lousy trap ... and there are the weak-minded who enjoy this revolting spectacle'. The political question is whather there is a need for a Jewish soveriegn State. Fathi believes not. Come the Arab victory, and at the head of the Haifa port administration 'there will be an Arab, and a Jew will act as deputy'. Most Jews will leave for more hospitable shores. They are, in political terms, 'a transient phenomenon'. The others remaining will constitute a tolerated minority. For those on the other side of the ideological divide, this picture, apart from being an illusory construct, is one of disaster, negating the whole necessary Zionist venture.

The success of this book lies in its ability to marry the political with the personal and social situations of the characters. At each point, we learn sufficient of the background of the people involved to grasp their motivation, and see how ideology is both reflected in their thinking and feeling, and then itself reflects it. The war, the decisive moment, sharpens and sometimes resolves it. But there is constant tension and uncertainty. Will Shula and Fathi finally get together and activate their mutual sexual attraction? It certainly looks possible. But the novel ends at this point of potential contact, when Fathi is about to leave, only pausing to ask Shula to accompany him to Jenin (he needs the security of Arab soil), and even marry him. But it does not happen; 'At that moment, they stopped being man and woman. He was just an Arab, and she, just a Jewess'. If, in spite of the blend of personal and political contours, one can still divide the novel into these two levels, one might say that here, finally, the political triumphs over the personal. In this sense, this is a political novel. It ambitiously tackles the political crux of the State of Israel, its most dire problem with its historical roots and awesome implications. But it does not dissolve into bombast, nor lose perspective. We never forget that there are real people involved, and we see the way that they are coloured by the political brush.

חסות *Hasuth* is by no means a major novel, neither stretching imaginatively the techniques of Hebrew fiction, nor creating a new dynamic of its own. It is, however, a very good book, tightly written, authentic and exciting within its own limitations. The author has etched a world with a dialectic that he himself has clearly known and experienced. And it is an important world.

* * *

קרקס הפרעושים *QIRQAS HAPAR'OSHIM* (The Flea Circus, 1977) by Mordekhai Horowitz

Within the scope and variety of the Israeli novel, its experimentation in types of narrative, in disguises, in symbolism and allegory, it has been weak in that area which had been the novel's original function. It has not produced a great deal of social realism. The picaresque narrative, where a single hero tries to pick his way through a hostile environment, meeting difficulties to overcome them, and eventually triumphing, has been retailed by Agnon, but not much otherwise. Mordekhai Horowitz makes such an attempt here, deliberately unfolding a large canvas of Israeli society, particularly in the cogs and wheels of its industrial and commercial infrastructure, against which the bold hero (here, the first person narrator), is buffeted. This hero succeeds within the system, (having qualified as a lawyer, he then abandons his profession and works his way up from a lowly position in a commercial company) but then, as appropriate to the terms proposed by the novel, that system is rejected in favour of something much grander. The hero, now in his late thirties, after experimentation as a private writer, must now devote his life to the overriding function of 'artist'. He must be a writer in Israel, the new Jew against the backdrop of a resurrected Israel, product of four thousand years of Jewish existence. And his function is to describe that scene, and more, to show that a tiny nation can be of greater significance than the numerically and politically awesome states in the rest of the world. This is the narrator of the long novel in the picaresque mood, holding up his small objects for satire and obloquy, or promoting proponents of his great idea.

The objects of his satire are the petty-bourgeois, the small-minded, those obsessed with minor (*sub specie aeternitatis*) social concerns, their career prospects and progress, their status and their position within a corrupted world. Proponents of his great idea are such as Bahbut, the Moroccan-French visitor, with whom the narrator lives for a while, and himself. These two are concerned, obsessed, with the notion of the Jew. In fact, Bahbut seems to be a projection of the narrator himself. Early in the novel, the narrator is too self-effacing to deliver himself of the reams of bombast that single Bahbut out as an unusual genius. But then Bahbut is dismissed, at which point the narrator can take over. The picaresque novel should be a novel of self-discovery and growth, where the world helps the hero in his maturation and self-fulfillment. In קרקס הפרעושים *Qirqas Hapar'oshim*, it seems that our hero Ben-Ari does come to the realisation of his own splendid distinction. He is aware now of how superior he is to the masses dotted around in the public places: 'My God, my God, why hast Thou forsaken me in this world full of chimpanzees enjoying the exploitation of possibilities for their own sake?' In that same context, we are made aware of how the hero sees himself: 'The Passion of St. Ben Ari within this filth is still to be written'. This he observes on hearing a version of St. Matthew's Passion from a pedestrian's transistor radio on Dizengoff Street.

What we have here is an angry, satirical novel, within which the hero, on his voyage of self-discovery within the contemporary, urban Israeli scene, comes, sees, conquers and then rises above the unworthy throng. It must be asked whether the satire is successful, particularly on such a scale. Successful satire must contain two ingredients. Firstly, a point of view, from which the object of the satire is observed, held and castigated, that is adequate to such a purpose. Secondly, a technique sufficient for its expression in invention, with and consistency. As for the first, it must be said that although the work is not lacking in stamina or explicitness, the only clear recognition transmitted by the narrator is of his own superiority. This would seem to be an insufficient condition for the sort of major satire aspired to here. The social critique is trivial, the objects castigated are unworthy, the targets are too easy. And the second weakness springs precisely from the first condition. Having selected such easy targets for his shafts of 'irony', the narrator proceeds to expend on them not arrows but heavy explosives. He creates scenes that could conveivably succeed in miniature, but then blows them up to grotesque proportions, inflating his targets well beyond the capacity they naturally fill. His illiterate girl-friend Sura is awarded dozens of pages, and the reader has to have not only her dialogue, but the superior reflections of Ben-Ari himself about everything said. In the way of the picaresque novel, there are many separate scenes and incidents recorded here, but they are arbitrary, without a connecting spine, and clumsily drawn. And there are various loose ends not brought together.

Ben-Ari is a hero with some of the ambitions recorded in Fielding's *Tom Jones* but with none of the nice observation or invention, with apparently some of the seething hatred for humanity recorded by Swift, but with little of the wit. These are comparisons unfortunately invited by the book itself in its disproportionate pretension. Bahbut is drawn (presumably not intentionally) as a windy, bombastic Zorba, preaching the life force: 'Learn to live, learn to enjoy the small things that life has to offer'. But he is also a tired Zorba, whose claim to any sort of attention is only supported by the declared reverence of those who surround him. Of course, he is much given to extreme moods and extravagant whims, but these are not integrally tied to the central thread of a controlling personality. This character, thankfully, moves further into the background in the course of the narrative, but the bombast and pretence are henceforth assumed by the narrator. The narrator must then become the spokesman of that 'historical organism', the Jewish people, a task that Bahbut had seen as his own. He says of himself, 'I became a maniac for Judaism and Jews'. But this noble purpose is unmatched by any transmitted relation to Jewish history or existence. We just have to take the author's word for it. Ben-Ari's pretension becomes, in his view, his achievement. And anyone who doubts the worthiness of the pretension or the genius of its potential expression, is a materialistic Philistine.

Interesting indeed is the way in which the narrator sees himself and his intense relationship to Jewish existence. As spokesman of a parallel attitude, though, of course, not in regard to the Jews, he selects, rather inappropriately, Henry Miller, that wonderful voice of the urban alienated. And he quotes, appropriating the sentiment for the Jews, 'Underneath, below the deepest foundations, there lies another race of men. They are dark, sombre, passionate. They muscle into the bowels of the earth. They wait with a patience that is terrifying. They are scavengers, the devourers, the avengers. They emerge when everything topples into dust'. This, for Ben-Ari, is an analogue of the Jews, waiting in the wings for the collapse of a rotten European civilisation. And Israel, resurrected in recent years, expresses that possibility: 'To know that two and a half million Jews in a sovereign State constitute a first range world power, to know that we have no connection with the rottenness of Europe'. Israel, for the Jews, is 'rebirth towards a brilliant future'. The thesis is more than entrancing. It is provocative. But unfortunately, it is then confused. Because this rottenness apparently not only attaches itself to European Christians, but to the Jews within those lands too. Ben-Ari's senior colleague, Arazi, himself of German origin, utters a long diatribe relating to the natives of Germany and the implications of German education. He avows that German Jews are capable of greater and more total evil than the non-Jews. The Christians have, after all, managed to express their destructive intent. With the Jews, it is all potential, and thus bottled-up, awaiting its moment, In what is presumably a reference to Kissinger's Middle Eastern role, Arazi says that one day, someone of German-Jewish origin will rise to significant power in America, and then complete Hitler's work, with even greater devastation and scientific finality. But, if this is so, what of the basic thesis? Are the Jews not then a separate and uninfected entity? Or does this apply only in Israel? In these blighted and nasty streets, with their drab population? He does after all say; 'This State of Israel, which has murdered the Land of Israel, has always bored me'. The answer then must be that sole salvation is in the hands of that unique conqueror, Ben-Ari himself. Unfortunately, though, we are not quite sure how it is to be accomplished, or, even more elementarily, what should be accomplished. A windy statement of contempt and self-superiority is no substitute for analysis, structural competence, character portrayal or nice wit.

The sad thing is that there was so much more potential here; potential both for narrative and for satire. Perhaps the author has been too carried away by the need to say everything, to put all down, to give vent to all sorts of frustrations, major and minor, personal as well as ideological, to pay more than scant regard to the proper taste of the novelist. Had it been pared down and then very considerably understated, the kernel of קרקס הפרעושים *Qirqas Hapar'oshim* might have then made a more striking entrance. Of course, some of the redemptive function would have had to be jettisoned. But there has to be trouble with a narrator who can place himself so without irony at the fulcrum of existence. This is said when he begins to appreciate the necessity of his new function as full-time writer, and emerges into the light of day: 'For so long was I down below and outside, that mankind ceased to be ashamed before me ... I now know what 'mankind' is in a way that very few people know'. The trouble is that he has been telling us. Quite another possibility is that the whole book is a narrative irony; that Ben-Ari, like his friend Gumperz, self-styled 'King of the Jews', is not sane, at least in the eyes of the outside world. But this does not take us much further in a consideration of the text.

קרקס הפרעושים *Qirqas Hapar'oshim* can serve as an object lesson in the possibilities of the Israeli novel. Both satire and the novel as a genre emanate from a particular society and Israeli society would be well rewarded with good satirical narrative. But such narrative would be better served too, if quasi-mystical claptrap were omitted. This particular combination of personal confession, commercial and sexual adventures, together with spiritual exploration, has been attempted before, and in the Israeli novel too, as in Sadeh's early work.[2] But the pitfalls have not been removed. The attempt to produce such a work should still be made.

[2] And in Dan Ben-Amotz's recent novels.

9

ENTRY INTO A TANGLED ORCHARD:
CONCLUSIONS IN THE
CONTEMPORARY ISRAELI NOVEL

Every defined thing comes to an end; every artifact has a stop;
every work of art aspires to completion. The very ending of a
work guarantees a sense of psychological wholeness.

The ending fulfiles a spiritual need—it leads to a healing of a
breach or to a release of tensions.[1]

We can learn something about the nature of the contemporary Israeli novel by examining its endings. The end closes
the circle and completes the destiny outlined in the preceding
account.

A frequent phenomenon in the Israeli novel of recent years is
the flight of the protagonist from the grey everyday reality that
surrounds him. The hero in the story aspires to break through
the wall, or to flee from the environment around, or to take off
to the heights. Or the narrator introduces a comment from the
outside, raising the described reality to another level. This
tendency can already be seen in Yoram Kaniuk's היורד למעלה
Hayored lma'alah (The Acrophile, 1961) where the narrator hides
on top of a skyscraper in New York so as to look down on
humanity from on high, from the top of its own fortress. In the
books of Pinhas Sadeh, the hero creates a world of his own
which ignores the external world and surpasses it in terms of the
absolute values it embodies— החיים כמשל Hahayim kemashal (Life
as a Parable, 1958),[2]— על מצבו של האדם Al matzavo shel ha'adam
(The Human Condition, 1967) and others. In Sadeh's work the
individual is presented as a deviant, and in this way the human
experience is reinforced.

*
* *

Here I will look at several examples of endings from novels
that appeared in the late 60s and early 70s.

In Yitzhak Orpaz's מסע דניאל Masa Daniel (Daniel's Journey,
1969), the protagonist who returns from the war goes through a

[1] See Barbara Hernstein-Smith, *Poetic Closure* (Chicago, 1968).
[2] *Life as a Parable*, London, 1966.

spiritual crisis. At the centre of the occurrences stands the figure of Aphrodite, the goddess who is always born anew. The sea is the axis of the events and the key to the change in Daniel's character. This tendency to overuse symbols appeared in Orpaz's earlier works, עור בעד עור *Or be'ad or* (Skin for Skin, 1963), מות ליסנדה *Moth Lisanda* (Death of Lysanda, 1966),[3] and נמלים *Nemalim* (Ants, 1968). In מסע דניאל *Masa Daniel*, when the hero returns from the war all he hears all the time is the sea. He not only hears, he also listens to it. This activity accentuates his separation from conventional society, from his family and his friends. Only this heightened consciousness interests him; 'And he really had to strain his ears to hear the sound of the sea in the middle of the day through the din of the streets, the people, the cars, the words'. He aspires to something beyond this, and flees from the reality of the war, the ugly reality 'To penetrate, to penetrate the womb of the sea!' he declares, seeing the sea as the mother that has given him birth. He returns to his city, Tel Aviv, as to a kind of Messiah. And the story concludes with the description of a party. He recalls the question that the girl Rachela, has asked him; what, in his view, is the most important thing in life? He muses about this as he touches her head and the novel concludes with words that reflect his thoughts: 'What a wonder, each single hair'. His vision is strengthened and from now on concentrates on each wondrous detail.

* * *

The question of the real and the supra-real occurs in החיים הקצרים *Hahayim Haqtzarim* (The Short Life, 1972) by Aharon Megged. Dr Elisheva Tal-Blumfeld, a literary critic and scholar, hardly distinguishes life from literature. With regard to literature, she casts grave doubts on the 'realistic' approach. And when she tries to realise her literary theory in life, she flees to a transcendent reality. Here, Megged returns to the protagonist's desire for an independent life, as he expressed it in החי על המת *Hahay 'al hameth* (The Living on the Dead, 1965). Even the existence of the central figure in מחברות אביתר *Mahbroth evyathar* (Evyatar's Notebooks, 1974) is problematic. The riddle central to this book is, why Richter, the great writer, retains such

---

[3] *The Death of Lysanda*, London, 1970.

strong hatred for Eviatar, the narrator. The ending is open: 'And maybe, I think, all this is nothing but the revenge he's taking on me for leaving him without his permission, for leaving him alone with his manuscripts, with his stories? Revenge and payment for my only sin towards him'. Here the narrator points to a liberation from a burden, but the escape is not complete and its effectiveness is doubtful.

* * *

Binyamin Tammuz's יעקב *Yaaqov* (Jacob, 1971) as its title might suggest questions the identity of the people of Israel, and the topic returns in symbolic form in הפרדס *Hapardes* (The Orchard, 1972). Two men walk into the one orchard, but to which of the two does it belong? The book deals with the legal ownership of the desired orchard, i.e. Eretz Israel. Two brothers claim it, one a Jew and one an Arab. And what is the solution to this highly topical problem? The book concludes as follows: 'New people will come gleefully to live in the new houses. And after a generation or two these people too will also be dust and ashes. And the houses too will crumble. And in my mind's eye, I see resurrection and destruction, destruction and resurrection, and it all has no end. Until the solver of riddles come and solve this riddle too at the end of days'. Here is a concentration of messianic and religious concepts, and it is difficult to see how the story supports them. The *pardes* (region of speculation, four methods of Biblical interpretation, that area so difficult to navigate), or orchard, is an area of dangerous, even forbidden, contemplation. Resurrection is the climax of the vision of Ezekiel. The end of days is the end of this world of ours as we know it and verges on the threshold of messianic times. And who is the solver of riddles if not the God of Israel? But can such terms stand in their own right in a secular context? The narrator finds reality hard to digest, and turns his back on it.

* * *

Amos Oz's לגעת במים לגעת ברוח *Laga'ath bamayim laga'ath baru'ah* (Touch the Water, Touch the Wind, 1973) also deals with the national topic of the greater Israel, i.e. the State of Israel together with World Jewry. Mr Pomeranz and his wife arrive in Israel by different and devious routes. The couple separates a number of times but in the end is finally reunited on the soil of Eretz Israel. To be more precise, not just *on* the soil of Israel but within it, for they are swallowed up in the earth by an incredible earthquake. Here are the familiar features of Oz's writing; the sense of siege, desire, destructive passion, ecstasy, etc. The summation is the sociological character of our lives— smooth surface, unstable foundation. The book ends in an attempt to unite the various and diverse elements, all of which reach their climax at the conclusion of the story, and blend together; we read of the funeral of Ernst, the kibbutz secretary, of Yotam and Audrey (the younger generation) crossing the border (they are seeking 'urgent salvation'), and of the chant sung by the older couple, the Pomeranzes. Finally, a crack opens in the earth, the couple is swallowed up, and the melody of their chant fades. The closing lines envisage the years to come: 'But during those evening hours the large lights are already burning in the recreation building, and from the illumined hall a different music rises and pours outwards'.

This allusion to a 'different music' hints also at a different world, one that is distinct from present reality, but is not defined. In this novel music and mathematics are symbols of perfection. Realia and allegory mix together.

These writers are much concerned with whatever lies beyond death. Aharon Appelfeld's favourite topic is the tight thread which can be woven between two people and which can become an unseverable link. The past exists in the present. In his novel העור והכתנת *Ha'or wehakuthoneth* (The Skin and the Shirt, 1971), this link exists not only for the duration of life but also holds after death. Here is the ending of the novel, the narration of the thoughts of Gruzman after the death of the old woman Betti: 'And all night he walked about as after a funeral, on a journey into which penetrated, slowly, like hard drops of poison, the memory of their first meeting. And this was like a lighted corridor, even before the words sprouted, in the feverish transition to a sleep which brought nothing. It occurred to him that this was death. At first the body dies, and then the soul goes on boiling until it too evaporates and the winds gather it up with the first red hues of dawn'.

*   *

Dan Ben-Amotz is a writer who responds to current issues in the State of Israel. His novel *Lo sam zayin* (Don't Give a Damn, 1973), is a most topical book which treats of youth in revolt against the background of local reality. A young man wounded in a military operation tries to bring the consciousness of the wounded to the public at large, and fails. But despite its everyday and up-to-date subject matter, the book finally evades a confrontation with the situation. The young man, Rafi, stands beside the bereaved old man, a pleasant, gentle character. They are both high on drugs, because, as Rafi puts it, a purple pill makes life easier. They float in the sky and they feel good, because this way they're hidden from the ugly reality. The crippled Rafi, who finds no solution in his confrontation with the real, claims, 'The purple's good too. It throws you, and you fly, you're in the sky! ... I can't walk, but to fly—that's so easy! Like in dreams'. He takes a tone similar to that in מסע דניאל *Masa' Daniel*. It is better to be in the sky among angels and dreams than to be fixed to the earth.

* * *

Shulamit Har-Even, in עיר ימים רבים *'Ir yamim rabim* (City of Many Days, 1973), concludes her story in a similar way, though the tone and direction are different. In her presentation of Jerusalem—the city of many days,—she gives a clear characterisation of the place and of the relation of the family to it. Here too the place points to the beyond. The present moment hints beyond itself, and one who lives in this city touches the sky. Sarah's thoughts were, 'This whole city lay before her and she looked at the gentle light ... As if once, long ago, close to the creation of the world, some great stone had cracked and all the truth inside it has flowed out radiant onto these slopes. She sensed the moment with all her being ... Now I'm contained in that moment ... I can walk in it, slowly. I can touch the sky—it's so close now. To breathe mountain and light, now'. Here is a mixture of nowness and eternity. But the atmosphere is somewhat different to that which rises from the pages of לא שם זין *Lo sam zayin*, for instead of an effort on the part of the characters to flee and to take off to the heights, here the sky is brought down to the earth.

* * *

There are other possibilities for conclusions too. Nathan Shaham's הלוך ושוב *Halokh washov* (Return Journey, 1972), for example, still places the weight of the book on its ending. He tries, through the eyes of the young widow who is his protagonist, to embrace the totality of experience abroad as a proof of the necessary centrality of Israel. In doing this, Shaham continues his path as a political-moralistic author, and the climax of the moralism comes at the end of the novel, when Liat, the widow, returns to Israel, to her family, and to her dying father-in-law. 'Yoav's father died of a heart-attack several days after her return. She only managed to see him once. They spoke of the memorial booklet (for Yoav). His happiness was wonderful to see. As if to say, her return had mended something. As if it had become clear to him that the youth of today was not shaking off responsibility. Which meant that life would not lessen in his absence'. Here there is no escape, no flight from or floating above the described world. On the contrary, there is a king of attempt to close a circle by reconcilation with the situation. The hero finds the remedy in the girl's return, in the natural course of events.

* * *

Amalia Kahana-Carmon, in וירח בעמק אילון *Weyareah be'emeq Ayalon* (The Moon in the Valley of Ayalon, 1971), suggests another way of ending a novel. In line with her translation of the unconscious and fragmented levels of human relationships, she shortens the conclusion, or leaves it open, narratively incomplete. This is also the form that speech takes in her stories, the way the central figure gropes for confrontation with the world, and so too is it the story as a whole. Self-knowledge is always partial. The story imitates life. Thought flows through the brain, and writing tries to grasp it. The heroine of this novel tries to define herself, and reads about a preparation for an imaginary interview. What she reads appears to her to be the story of her life. The interview in the manuscript does not take place, and here are the last lines of the story: 'What do you think you've just read, Mr Hiram takes the sheets from Mrs Talmor's hands, and gravely puts them into a paper bag. / The story of my life—she thought, shocked, as usual. / Not finished yet, he waves his hand in dismissal'. The book concludes with an admission of its incompleteness, because it pretends to tell about the life of its heroine.

133

* *

These are some of the diverse ways in which the modern
Israeli novel ends. But the conclusion always seems to attempt
to fulfil a spiritual need and offer completion. It drives towards
its end according to the assumptions that compel the story itself.
But sometimes the conclusion separates itself from the sequence
of the story and aspires to something else, even to an all-
encompassing generalisation, and does not remain faithful to
the data of the story. Two directions can be seen here; a thrust
towards generalisations and a tendency to mysticism. Many of
these novels conclude with a flight to the skies, and in so doing
they express an attempt to liberate themselves from the chains
of the story.

There is nothing defective in the existence of a mystical
approach *per se*, if it stems naturally from the schemes established in the story, but a *deus ex machina* imposed upon the story
may shake up the credibility of the work as a whole. The reader
is after all not the solver of riddles, and he will not be able to
find the suitable solution. The responsibility remains with the
author—to find the bricks suitable to his building. Sometimes
he succeeds.

10

THE JACKAL AND THE OTHER PLACE:
     THE STORIES OF AMOS OZ

Since the mid 60s, Amos Oz (born 1939) has been in the
forefront of Israeli fiction, both in popular regard and in critical
attention. He has produced a succession of stories, novellas and
novels [1] that have struck chords deep in the Israeli readership
and, through the medium of translation, abroad, where he has
won perhaps more notice than any other Israeli novelist. Each
work is striking in incident, character, plot and viewpoint,
though, as we shall see, there have been changes of course
over the years of the œuvre. Psychological insight has been
combined with dramatic tension and narrative sophistication to
create a disconcerting resonance. The mood is often extreme,
some might think, wayward, the incidents often unhappy or
cruel, some might think sadistic, the psychological terminology
regular, some might think monotonous or limited. But there is a
subtlety of effect in the depiction of the human condition that
always suggests disturbing, normally unsuspected layers of
construction in the specifically Israeli condition too. The cliché
of Israeli society is not left unchallenged, as its pathology is
exposed to the exploratory probing of a restless pen.

In an interview given to an Israeli newspaper,[2] Oz was
invited to speculate on the possibility of a Middle East peace in
the wake of the Sadat initiative. If there should be peace for
Israel, how would this affect the literature of the country? Oz

---

[1] The bound volumes of his work are: ארצות התן *Artzoth Hathan* (a
collection of short stories written between 1962 and 1965, when they were
published together. The volume was then revised and republished with an
additional story in 1975): מקום אחר *Maqom Aher* (a novel, 1966); מיכאל שלי
Mikhael Sheli (a novel, 1968); עד מוות *Ad Maweth* (two novellas, 1971);
ארבעה פרקים ראשונים *Arba'ah Praqim Rishonim* (four chapters of what is
now a completed novel, published in the Davar newspaper 1972 and then in
the anthology of his work אנשים אחרים *Anashim Aherim*, 1974); לגעת במים
לגעת ברוח *Laga'ath Bamayim Laga'ath Baruah* (a novel, 1973); הר העצה הרעה
Har Haetzah Hara'ah (three novellas, 1976); באור התכלת העזה *Be'or Hath-
kheleth Ha'azah* (collection of essays, 1979). סומכי *Sumkhi* (a children's story,
1980). מנוחה נכונה *Menukhah Nekhonah* (a novel, 1982 — developing the
"four chapters" published in 1972).
[2] *Ma'ariv*, 30.12.77.

both answers the question by suggesting that the writer might revert to his normal concern and also asserts the constant centrality of the negative in a writer's work. There is always something going wrong, whatever the larger political reality: 'Children will not understand their parents well, parents won't understand their children. Brothers and sisters will sometimes fight, men and women won't get on particularly well even if there is peace. And as for the weak people, the little men, the sufferers and the afflicted—literature will treat of them. Perhaps there will also be a literature dealing with heroes, but that's hard for me to believe'. Literature, avers the writer, has a tendency to treat the negative. That is where its strength seems to be located: 'A story about despair can be finer than despair itself, a poem about death less painful than death'. The observed corollary is that literature does not seem to excel in descriptions of the magnificent or the successful. In such instances, the thing described is always finer in reality, and literature falls short of its model. Literature then seems to be the cathartic transformer of the negative into something worthwhile in its own right, an art work.

* *

It is from the base of this description of literature's function that we can begin to delineate the contours of Oz's writing. We, of course, do not have to accept his characterisation as a universal truth holding good for all work, in order to see how it works for him. The question posed to him as an Israeli writer who has grown up in a political and social condition of siege, and whose work noticeably (in the view of critics) bears that scar and image, is, if the external condition of siege is lifted, will this not necessarily affect the character of the literature produced in the changing society? And if this is so, how will this change operate? Oz answers by saying that scarred literature is not a product of an external political influence, but rather an internal necessity. Shakespeare, writing at a splendid period of English history, is not at his greatest in his celebration of glory. He might have said that this human condition is necessarily tragic. So if the threat does not come from without, it would still spring from within.

Threat is a major theme of Oz's stories. The name of his first collection, ארצות התן *Artzoth hathan* (Lands of the Jackal, 1962, also the title story), embodies just that. Because the 'jackal' is actuality and symbol. In the prophet Jeremiah's words, when Jerusalem is destroyed it will be מעון תנים 'a habitation of jackals' (Jeremiah 10:22), there used in parallel with 'wasteland'. The jackal represents the threat constantly, in the wings, waiting to pounce and tear. In Oz's stories, the very landscape acquires the character of extreme emotion described. The onset of autumn in the title story makes the fields 'quake'.

But the character of the threat is ambivalent. It is dangerous but also fascinating. Pain is also desired. In the story, Gelilah is both fascinated and terrified by Damkov. When she remembered his invitation 'she was filled with revulsion and gaiety. She thought of his gripping ugliness ...' Revulsion is paired with gaiety, ugliness with an exciting quality. And this is the dual nature ascribed to persons, animals and the general situation. The narrative description deliberately breaks down the borderline between the animate and the inanimate. Atmosphere is invested with a live quality, as the animal (jackal or snake) takes on a human colour. He writes here, 'The tender violet light wraps the treetops with great mercy ... removes the distance between mineral and animal'. The light has a transformative power, it gives everything 'a cold seething quake, a quake of poison'. The thing that attracts is also deadly, and, on certain occasions, as when this light prevails, 'we cannot descry the jackals emerging from their burrows'. So even if the most terrible danger is close, one might be unaware of it. The animal parallel is brought out explicitly by Damkov to Gelilah, when he tells her of breeding horses, 'At that moment, there is no difference between pleasure and pain. The copulation is very like castration'. Then comes a description of a trapped jackal. Caught by the trap, it begins to lick the metal 'as though spreading warmth and love over the object'. These opposite poles might pose a confusion, so the author suggests a unifying element at the story's conclusion: 'If you want a fixed point in the stream of time and seasons, you should listen to the sounds of the night which never change. These sounds come to us from there'.

The title story is not the only one in the volume which dwells on an ambivalent relationship of extremes. Similar images recur throughout. It takes its most dramatic form in נוודים וצפע *Nawadim Watzefa* (The Nomad and the Viper), when we have two encounters described on the part of the girl Geulah, one with a Bedouin Arab and the other with a viper. The Arab is

137

described by her as possessing a 'repulsive beauty'. The viper approaches Geulah after she has been thinking of coming to terms with the Arab. The reasons for her flight are doubtful. She rests. Had she already been bitten that she needs to lie down? Is she bitten now? And what is the feeling? 'The pain is dim, almost delightful'. And at the end of the story 'her fingers caress the dust and her face is very tranquil almost beautiful'. We assume that the worst has happened, and yet the climax seems to reverse normal expectations. The snake parallels the situation of the Arab who is dangerous (particularly to her; did he rape her?). And both dangers are also alluring.

Threat is one of the chief elements in מיכאל שלי *Mikhael Sheli* (My Michael, 1968) too. As in Oz's stories, the pervasive sense of threat is awarded concrete reality in a specific image. Hannah, the narrator in the novel, is obscurely discontented, troubled by unarticulated disturbances and aspirations. The parallel to the snake/Arab of 'The Nomad and the Viper' is the pair of twins whom she had apparently known from childhood. They are indeed very sinister: '... and the dreams. Hard things are intended for me each night. Towards morning the twins practise with hand grenades amongst the crags of the Judean desert ...' This might be a threat to her personally, to Israel in general, or it might even be the universal danger that everyone carries around within himself. Certainly Jerusalem, where most of the story takes place, is so threatened: 'Villages and suburbs close on Jerusalem a tight ring, like people standing curious around an injured woman cast to the ground: Nabi Samuel, Shaafat, Sheikh Jarah, Augusta-Victoria'. Jerusalem is like a woman, like Hannah. The hills are like the twins. What they inflict, as in Hannah's later fantasies of rape by the twins, is 'trembling thrills of pain running down, igniting to the palms'. The novel concludes with one of the recurrent visions of the twins. The jackal is there too: 'It breaks out, cries, and is silent'. There is 'a caress redolent of longing'. The last phrase is 'And over great expanses descends a cold tranquility'. The author continually holds the reins of the opposite qualities, suggesting the ambivalent view of the subject towards the source of danger.

* * *

Oz's fiction could be otherwise described as the fiction of extreme situations. Occasionally, the author seems to break into the story in the guise of a narrator commenting on his own art. In נוודים וצפע *Nawadim Watzefa*, the 'I' of the narrative comments on Geulah's reactions to his (i.e. the narrator's) own stories, 'She does not like my stories because of the extreme polarisation of situations, landscapes and figures: the intermediate shades between light and darkness are lacking'. This must be an ironic comment. The very person who is dismissive of such states then surrenders herself to them. She it is who courts the danger of the Bedouin and the snake and who then is ambiguously caught by both, trapped in the oxymoron of 'the pain ... almost delightful'. She it is too who noted 'the repulsive beauty' of the Arab, and who then got involved with him. This could not be an accident. In Oz's work, the plot is the external exemplification of unconscious motivation. The story דרך הרוח *Derekh haruah* (Way of the Wind) recounts in considerable and gruesome detail the disastrous parachute jump of an inexperienced youngster, who gets caught in electric wires and fried. Paradoxically, the incident opens with an analysis of pleasure, the wonderful sensation involved in such a jump. Such pleasure is of two types—abandoned pleasure and restrained pleasure. The first is gained initially at the moment of jumping when the body is totally surrendered to the elements. The second is achieved when the parachute is opened, and countervailing force is introduced against the elements, exercising some degree of control. Gideon is unprecedently excited by the total experience: 'Never in his life had he tasted a love so strong and thrilling. All his muscles tensed, and a sort of spring of delight gushed in his strength and through his back up to the neck and the roots of his hair'. His courage fails him at the critical moment and his lack of experience and competence bring about a disaster. His own father, who is also the spiritual father of the kibbutz (a common figure in Oz's stories) is also subject to a duality of emotion. His shame at the ineptitude of his son is modified by paternal grief in bereavement. The weather at this moment, a khamsin which will surely recur, reinforces the general mood. This is the movement between extremes.

Another character that makes frequent appearance in Oz's stories is the one who foresees disaster. The story תקון העולם *Thiqun ha'olam* (Repair of the World) is a sort of memorial to such a person, an extreme ideologue, on his death.) As so often with our author, he is viewed ambivalently. The narrator introduces him as someone who 'all his life has lived in hatred'.

But we are assured that the members of the kibbutz view him rather as a fervent upholder of an uncompromising ideological position. The ironic view of kibbutzniks, also to come to the fore in מקום אחר *Maqom Aher* (1966), is of people who do not believe in the negative, in this case, hatred. Evil is generally explained away by such types as expressions of an imperfect system or of ideological extremism. These are people who would improve things, who repair the world; the subject of the story is the ultimate of this type. But we are reminded that the burial of such a person (and his death too) does not differ in character from the burial of anyone else. It is the essential quality of the human condition that keeps coming through so insistently. The facts of life persist, whatever local conditions prevail, or whatever efforts are made to effect change. We are presented with an account from three sides, from the point of view (as it were) of the deceased, from the point of view of his colleagues (he had no family or close friends) and from the point of view (implied) of the ironic observer/author. All suggest ambiguity.

But a whole novella is devoted to an account of the prophet of doom, אהבה מאוחרת *Ahavah Meuhereth* (Late Love) from the volume עד מות *Ad Maweth* (1970). There, the subject tells his own story in his own words, but the reader must needs draw his own conclusions. He, Shraga Ungar, is obsessed again with danger, and, as we have observed in Oz's other stories, the danger must take on specific form. The specific form of the danger perceived here by Ungar is that of the Soviet Union which has conspired totally against the Jews. It is now Ungar's sole function in life to bring this knowledge to the awareness of his fellow Jews so that they can take preventive measures: 'The Bolsheviks, gentlemen', he says in one of his often repeated addresses, 'have made a secret decision to liquidate the whole Jewish people finally'. He also fantasises revenge on the part of the Jews against their baiters. Russia will collapse in the face of Jewish fury.

When we see such varieties of threat and danger, we do not have to challenge their specific character to recognise that they share common factors. And the quality held in common is a perception of the person, and the threat to him that may take on such various forms.

* * *

Such threat when it takes on specific garb suggests a further source of danger which is unspecific. But Oz's type of writing, with its polarity, also invokes an opposite. This opposite pole is the positive, the ideal and from what we have seen of the author's *ars poetica* we might guess that the positive pole is even cloudier than the negative. We are nor even sure of the character of the thing described. In the most allusive terms, an ideal is suggested beyond the experienced present, perhaps even beyond the expressible. This ineffable state is the 'other place' so often raised in Oz's work. His novel of that name מקום אחר *Maqom aher* (Another Place) adopts this phrase as a sort of recurrent motto. There are eleven appearances of the pair of words within the book, in very different contexts. The resonance of the phrase in fact is acquired through its intervention at odd points in the complex story. Noga, the young daughter of the poet-guide kibbutznik, imagines herself saying to Ezra the lorry driver; 'Some time in another hundred, in a thousand years time, you'll take me in your car and we'll go to another place'. In fact, the first use of the phrase is by Noga to Ezra when she hitches a lift with him on the kibbutz. He wants to put her down at the gate, but she suggests the possibility of 'somewhere else'. Herbert Segal, the kibbutz ideologue, is transported by music to 'another place'. Old man Berger, father of the three sons in the story is described as having 'his attention perhaps scattered in another place'. Reuben, speculating to his mistress Bronka about his daughter, suggests that 'she will go to another place', and then, in trying to make contact with Noga, tells her that she is in another place. Siegfried, Ezra's sinister brother living in Germany but on a visit to Israel, tells Reuben to go to another place. In the ironic (?) summary as spoken by the chorus (we), a sort of agreed kibbutz morality, the reader is invited to look at the present picture, and see 'not men and women who belong to another place', i.e. we are to concentrate on the delimited area precisely there. This suggestion might be ironic because the whole tone of the novel has constantly raised the possibility and the shadow of this other place. The conventional wisdom, the supposed first-person plural narrator of the story is contradicted by the story's own wayward development. Not all is the light and harmony preferred by that wisdom: 'We, according to our outlook, are opposed to darkness and the negative. Only out of some distortion in the soul can anyone prefer darkness to light'. Yet the reader is witness to just that negative victory. Reuben, the very apostle of light, is apparently defeated, in his conflict over his daughter's soul (quite Faustian) with Siegfried. Or so he is initially, at any rate. Nothing is totally simple. But a morality play is acted out, and things are not as they appear.

The sense of the 'other place' pervades many, maybe all, of the stories and characters of Oz. עד מוות *Ad maweth* considers the motives of the crusaders. They are, after all, also going to another place, to the Holy Land, and thereby 'to cleanse iniquities by the travail of travel'. Seen from the point of view of crusader zealots, the Jew is a daemonic force, disturbing the Christian search for religious ecstasy and achievement. They are looking for the Kingdom of Heaven. But again there is the ambivalence. They never arrive, and perhaps never can arrive. They are heading for Jerusalem, but their destination is not achieved. Because Jerusalem does not exist, at any rate, as a place, rather as 'pure love, not a place. They look rather to strip themselves of their bodies to become an evaporating mist'.

So the other place, for the kibbutznik as well as for the Crusader is not a visible destination which can be reached with the price of a travel ticket. Because the place, once reached, becomes evanescent. This is so for the Jew too in his traditional longing for Jerusalem. Kitya is told in הר העצה הרעה|*Har Ha'etzah Haraah* (1976), 'You have been on the way from Europe to Palestine for forty years. You'll never arrive. Likewise we've been going from the desert to Europe and we'll never arrive'. It seems that destinations are of such a character. Kumin's father in לגעת במים לגעת ברוח *Laga'ath Bamayim Laga'ath Baruah* (1973) is eventually allowed by his powerful son to spend his waning days in the land of his dreams in Palestine, but when he gets there 'there, in the longed-for Palestine, amongst hills and graves, then the old man sits and until his last, he does not cease to compose heartbreaking poems of yearning for some other Palestine, for the true one'. The true Palestine, the authentic promised land, is not the one that we can actually go to. There is, however, always another one, a heavenly Jerusalem.

* * *

Now we can see some of Oz's concerns and techniques whole, in their relationships to each other, rather than just in the localised context. There is firstly an ironic interplay between actuality, the specific event, and what is represented by that actuality, the shadowy beyond. We are left in no doubt that, on the one hand, we are supposed to see the things that we do see in all their particular colours and contours. But we are also, on the other, in no doubt that there is a deeper residue that is left after that particular reality has been exhausted. מקום. אחר *Maqom Aher* seems to be concerned precisely with this, the ambivalent relationship between the here and now, the kibbutz (some thought of it as a naturalistic novel on its appearance) and between the beyond, that 'other place', whose shape might be suggested by the hint of the opposite. The play is between reality and symbol. A similar tension is established in מיכאל שלי *Mikhael Sheli*. On the face of it we have a tale told by a woman reflecting on her relationship and marriage to a geologist. Yet each part suggests something further. Even the function of geologist describes the earth as something not finally formed and complete, but rather in process. Likewise is Jerusalem an ongoing condition rather than a finished product. Hannah, perhaps under the influence of her husband's profession, says, 'I too can sense secret forces restlessly scheming, swelling, pressing on the crust from within with restless powers'. Jerusalem, like any reality, is not merely what can be seen on the top surface.

Secondly, a central and constantly recurring image in Oz's writing is the border. This has particular significance for an Israel in a state of siege, where the geopolitical border is never far away, and where that border marks the divide between in and out, comradeship and murderous hostility. But there are other borders too, ones which can sometimes be easily traversed but which then re-establish their hold. In landscape descriptions, the parallel between the animate and inanimate is often suggested. Light, air, land, sky, hold destinies of men. Weather seems to partake of human passion. The jackal, sign of hostility, usually makes its appearance with the evening, near the border. Nature too can join forces with the enemy. At the end of the story מנזר השתקנים *Minzar hashatqanim* (Monastery of the Silent), we read: 'But quickly did the darkness betray those who placed trust in it. It gradually melted away from the tops of the Eastern hills, the lands of the enemy'. The border is still there. The border can have important psychological effects in the formation of character too as in the story על האדמה הרעה הזאת *Al ha'adamah hara'ah hazoth* (On This Evil Earth), where the Biblical judge/leader Jephthah's leadership qualities are much conditioned by his twilight condition of Amonite/Israelite. The story opens: 'Jephthah was born on the border of the desert. On the border of the desert too was dug his grave'. He belonged wholly to neither side, and thus could exercise dispassionate leadership. The distinction between Israel and neighbouring countries is indicated by Reuben acting as tourist guide at the opening of מקום אחר *Maqom Aher*; 'our' land is planned 'in an optimistic spirit'. It is symmetrical, worked-out and has a message. The hostile hills around about are sad, stark and unproductive.

Thirdly, the geological image is sometimes linked with the image of border. But whereas the border may be a man—made political division based on a particular situation and local expediency, the deeper structure of the earth is more significant and decisive. The kibbutz in מקום אחר *Maqom Aher* is situationally determined for all time (though, as we indicated, this situation is dynamic) by its geological features. It is placed in a narrow, long valley next to the Jordan river. These geological features breach the political divisions; the kibbutz is part of a land break which starts in Northern Syria. This could be a greater factor in the long term than temporary divisions. Hannah's inspection of her husband's work, apparently so dry, reveals the hidden powers that determine the world: 'Volcanic forces press from within'. This, both for her and for the novel as a whole, serves as a metaphor for her condition and the human condition. She may seem to be a very ordinary, well-adjusted young housewife, but things are going on inside her, invisible to anyone else, scarcely perceived even by herself, which do more to determine her fate than many more obviously external features. This may account for the ambiguity of situation in Oz's stories. What seems, wants, strives to be one thing is often invisibly forced to be another.

Fourthly, there is the battle undeclared in all Oz's stories. Forces of Light and Darkness are at war. מקום אחר *Maqom Aher* sets the fight on many fronts. Eva, Reuben's erstwhile wife, who leaves him for a tourist, Isaac Hamburger, to go and live in Munich, declares her view of Art: 'One should present the simple and great things like desire and death'. She is presumably the representative of the negative forces at work. Reuben's art is quite different, and he is a sort of official kibbutz poet. Reuben eventually moves into open conflict with Siegfried, Eva's representative, who has come for Noga. Both lose— Reuben in death, Siegfried in departure without Eva. We have in the novel various idyllic moments, such as the etching of Bronke's daughter-in-law in total contentment. But this sounds like irony. On the other hands, portraits of total evil, such as that of Oren Geva, sadistic and destructive, come over as they sound, realistic. There is a struggle between light and darkness, reason and unreason, both here and, for example, in מיכאל שלי *Mikhael Sheli*. There, Michael is the epitome of tolerance, good natured calculation, optimism, and Hannah is its opposite. She keeps doubting the meaningfulness of the word 'cause'. Things are arbitrary for her: 'The word cause always arouses complications and misunderstandings'. She is always aware of danger, threat, the twins, Jerusalem's unstable structure. Michael, on the other hand, she sees as concerned entirely for the future: 'As is the way with optimistic people, Michael regarded the present as formless, amenable matter which must be used to shape the future by hard, responsible work. The past was for him suspect'. The optimist looks forward, confident that he is potentially in control of all available matter with the means to hand. The pessimist/realist/negativist would not ascribe cause to events nor see things in symmetrical patterns, nor be confident of the ability of reason to inspire desired form and direction. Neither view is necessarily victorious in the working out of these stories, nor do we have a rigid line-up of forces. But that seems to be roughly what is happening.

* *

Some of the threads of the aspirations implicit in much of Oz's opus emerge in his most difficult novel לגעת במים לגעת ברוח *Laga'ath Bamayim Laga'ath Baruah* (Touch the Water, Touch the Wind). This novel is short, but more ambitious in scope and technique than his others. A thirty-year span is covered, continents traversed, both Diaspora and Israel considered. The novel opens with an account of the central character, Pomeranz, who, in the Poland of 1939, has to flee to the forests from the Nazis. This Pomeranz, a modest teacher, has ambitions not personal or material, but spiritual, and strives towards an absolute of 'pure spirituality'. His wife Stefa meanwhile stays behind. The old elements of threat still lurk in the story: 'And night like a heavy cloak crouches over the town of M ... clasping beneath it in a desperate embrace Jaroslaw Boulevard, the Concert Hall, the suburban wood huts, the guards in their menacing coats, the river, blackening the snow expanses, whispering forest to the city, and lo, the city became a forest'. The apposition of forest to city, the first representing barbarism, the second civilisation, is well known in Hebrew literature.[3] So the suggestion is that anarchy threatens the very bulwark of civilisation. And in the forest, too, danger threatens in a more extreme form. In a further use of the geological image, the author suggests the undermining of the elements: 'Beneath the crust of ice lurk forces that are not ice, far, far away from rest'. Pomeranz is trying to find his way in this savage environment, whose foundations are crumbling. Fortunately the war ends soon, and Pomeranz at a later stage can go to the Promised Land 'where Spring blooms eternal'. (He makes ironic use of a phrase from an early Bialik poem.) He tries to lead an exceedingly quiet life as a watchmaker, meanwhile pursuing his obsession with music and with infinity. His formula for the resolution of the paradox of infinity brings him world fame, and at a later stage, his wife Stefa, who has achieved seniority and responsibility in Soviet Party ranks, joins him on his kibbutz. In an eccentric climax to the story, during the Six-Day War, the couple finally united, play their mouth organs during the shelling, and the earth opens to take them in: 'There was a darkness over the Land and over the people. There occurred a surrender of the external earth crust with the rippling spasms at the moisture of warm lips, and slowly inwards, as through a virgin's lips, they were gathered in. The crack trembled a little longer then fell silent and closed over them with an unbelievable, tender silence, a dumb kiss of loneliness. The tune died out. The lawn returned to its calm form'. The novel ends with the observation that from the Public Hall of Culture on the kibbutz there emerges 'another music'.

The novel seems to treat the themes of breach and repair, Israel and Diaspora in Jewish history, music and mathematics (the idea of infinity) as an attempted solution to persistent problems. The novel is 'difficult' because of the radical departure from realism, beyond symbolism in fact, into a surrealistic whirlpool when unities are created out of all available divisions.

[3] See for example S. Y. Agnon's story ביער ובעיר *Baya'ar uva'ir* (In Forest and City) in the volume אלו ואלו *Elu Waelu*, where the forest is associated with rejection of the Torah and with licence.
[4] Later incorporated into מנוחה נכונה *Menukhah Nekhonah* (1980).

* * *

But this is not the sole direction in which Oz's work moves. The segment of a novel ארבעה פרקים ראשונים *Arba'ah prakim Rishonim* (1972), looked like a partial attempt to retell a kibbutz story in a more naturalistic manner than in מקום אחר *Maqom Aher*. We are introduced to two male characters, Yonathan Lipschitz, who had been on the point of leaving the kibbutz into which he had been born, and Azariah Gitlin, the young idealistic adventurer who wants to join the kibbutz, and act as a revitalising catalyst.

Oz's tendency towards the paring down of the emotional layers of the prose is discernible in the revisions made in the second edition of ארצות התן *Artzoth hathan*. More rarefied words are jettisoned, poetic forms modified, the relatively unusual verbal construction nithpael in which Oz had revelled, is generally modified either to the more common hithpael or to qal, verbal excesses such as overlaying plays on words, are reduced. He seemed to be searching at that stage for a more economical form of expression.

A further move in this apparent direction is made in the three stories of the volume הר העצה הרעה *Har Haetzah Hara'ah*, which are almost naturalistic in execution and effect. Interestingly enough, this naturalism takes as its subject matter the last days of the British Mandate in Palestine 1946-1947. So we see that the common background of these stories is the childhood recollection of the author who was born and grew up in the Jerusalem of that period. It seems, and this is confirmed by the *Ma'ariv* interview cited above, that in order to come as close as possible to a precise representation of actuality, he returns to childhood where events made their most lasting impact. These stories are a mixture of naturalism (wie es eigentlich gewesen ist), traditional Oz elements (the threat is still apparent in the description of, for example, the noman's land in Jerusalem: 'Beyond the low fence which Dad had built of iron pillars and old nets and painted in bright colours began no-man's land', and nostalgia. In fact, the third story of the collection is entitled געגועים *Ga'aguim* (Yearnings). Most of the title story takes place at the High Commissioner's house party. Hillel, the child, here appears in the third person, as he clearly cannot record events of which he has no knowledge (for example, the house party to which he was not invited). But the mood of despair in the father Hans is brilliantly etched. He compares the party to the last days of the Roman Empire. We are here dealing with another final burst, that of the British Mandate, and the feeling of ebbing glory is conveyed by the author who invokes all with a gentle nostalgia. The second story, אדון לוי *Adon Levi* (Mr Levy) is retailed by the child figure, and also vividly evokes the feeling of that time, the fierce sympathies of the child for extreme Jewish nationalism, the factional divisions, waning British rule, a moderate father and an ambivalent mother. And the third story, געגועים *Ga'aguim*, expresses itself in its title. It is a series of letters written by a dying doctor in Jerusalem to his erstwhile love just gone to America. The doctor is also torn between the symbolism and the actuality of Jerusalem.

The discussion of Amos Oz's work will be resumed in the final chapter with a consideration of מנוחה וכונה *Menukhah Nekhonah* (1982). There too the characters more between a naturalistic landscape and symbolic action. Inevitably, as the characters waver so does the narrative shift between two moods.

The Israeli novelist tries to make sense of his society. Whereas lyric poetry can directly relate the poet to himself, or to the Absolute, the novel is firmly located within the social world. Israel is an unusual case, not only because it has achieved statehood so recently, but also because it is, in the main, an immigrant society which yet claims a basic relationship to the geographical location in the Middle East as a source of nationhood. Thus the Israeli is in a situation of perplexity, unable to take his roots for granted as other nationals might do, and constantly having to define his connection with the country and the outside world, and then refine any original definition. A given society is always a difficult thing to grasp as the novelist rooted in a social context must grasp it. Israeli society has been additionally problematic, constantly changing its contours; new, yet historically ancient; multicoloured, unstratified in the way of other more static nations, but still challenging the novelist to offer his description and characterisation. The Israeli novelist must also place himself, as individual, within the map that he draws.

*
*   *

The writers of the generation of the State, i.e. of that generation which grew to adult awareness within the Israeli framework, were self-consciously 'Israeli'. A previous generation of Hebrew writers had deliberately sought out Israel, had acquired the Israeli landscape, had reshaped their learned Hebrew in accordance with the demands of a contemporary literary language. They were foreigners fulfilling an ideological imperative, aware of the problematic nature of their situation. The new writers were not selecting an option. They were, on the whole, growing up within Israel naturally, speaking Hebrew as their first language, and for the first time in centuries (as Hebrew writers), writing the language they were speaking. They lacked the layers of Hebrew literacy of which earlier Hebrew had been built. But they felt they could compensate with a new, ingrown familiarity, uncluttered by foreign models. They could relate directly to the land and language, and produce a new Hebrew literature reflecting this generation reared in Israel.

A typically Sabra prose writer of this generation was S. Yizhar, whose first story אפרים חוזר לאספסת *Ephraim hozer laaspeseth* (Ephraim Returns to the Lucerne, 1938) set the tone for all his later work. Yizhar operates in two genres—the short story and the long novel, ימי צקלג *Yemey Tziklag* (Days of Ziklag, 1958)—but both are composed of interior monologues on the part of the protagonists, mainly the hero, and a minimum of external action. Such a plot as exists serves to enable the protagonist to formulate his attitudes, and eventually reach a decision. The substance of the interior monologue is doubt, and the doubter is swayed by conformity with social norm on the one hand and conscience on the other. Most of Yizhar's stories were written in the wake of the War of Independence. The moral situation revolves around the action of soldiers and the propriety of certain courses of behaviour in time of battle. But even in his first story, this sort of approach is marked out. The central figure, a kibbutz member, wants to change the nature of his work, but is subject to pressure on the part of other members to remain where he is. Ephraim oscillates from one opinion to another, eventually adopting the line of least resistance and keeping his original employment. Social pressures win out, and the individual conscience is left to protest ineffectually.

Much of Yizhar's writing is devoted to landscape description. The landscape for Yizhar is the world, capable of absorbing the hero or alienating him. In השבוי *Hashavuy* (The Prisoner, 1948), the Israeli soldiers, about to take an Arab prisoner, are seen as the interlopers disturbing the scene: 'It seemed clear that it was impossible to penetrate further inside without arousing some excitement, and that immediately removed the purpose of the patrol'. The Arab prisoner, on the other hand, is an integral part of that landscape. Like an indigenous animal, he belongs. When taken, 'he descended from rock to rock between the shrubs as a shepherd descends between the shrubs with the startled sheep after him'. The weather, too, is hostile to the interlopers. The sun 'seemed to be a sort of high, dumb rebuke'. The narrator, the 'I' of the story, wants to release the prisoner and have nothing more of the affair. This presses on his conscience. But the weight of the other soldiers' opinion does not allow such an easy decision. The main part of the narration is taken up with the interior arguments of the narrator. And it ends indecisively; conscience loses, there is 'shameful helplessness'.

In other stories of Yizhar a key role is played by nature, the sounding board against which a character can hear and know himself. In שיירה של חצות *Shayarah shel hatzoth* (Midnight Convoy, 1950), only one character of the story, Zviyaleh, can be properly absorbed into his surroundings: 'Of them all, only Zviyaleh was lying stretched out, warming his belly on the softened clods, removing himself from the conversation, from the stirring and from everything, going out to himself, gliding pleasurably, escaping silently into the world's expanses being opened round about; the more the sunset was being realised, the more he divested himself of his foreignness and could become graspable and understood'. Yizhar tries to describe the groping of his character to merge with his environment, which he does by introducing a springy, versatile (if somewhat heady and uncontrolled) Hebrew of wide vocabulary, deploying winding sentences and unusual structures, attempting to imitate the shape of the mind formulating its subtle nuances.

Yizhar has written very little fiction in recent years, but the material that has appeared in, for example, ספורי מישור *Sipurey Mishor* (Stories of the Plain, 1964) conforms to the lines indicated. One story, appropriately entitled ספור שלא התחיל *Sipur Shelo Hithil* (A Story Not Begun) has no plot at all, being a series of angry reflections back and forth. And another, הנמלט *Ha Nimlat* (The Runaway) relates only one piece of action; a action; a horse escapes and is recaptured. The first-person narrative voice is of a child who is deeply distressed by the plight of the horse. The feeling of elation is conveyed by the horse's escape, as is the disappointment following its recapture. This is the substance of Yizhar's stories; the individual's aspiration to freedom while seeking integration with the world, contrasted with his limited capacity and opposed by forces which finally vanquish and suppress this spirit.

* *

That Yizhar's powerful fictional voice has been gradually silenced is some indicator of the general mood of this literary generation. The Israeli world has changed so much that sometimes nostalgia has to be invoked to recreate it. This was done by Haim Guri (born 1923) also of this group, who composed such a exercise in הספר המשוגע *Hasefer hameshuga* (The Mad Book, 1971). The tone of the book is adolescent, which is precisely what the writer is aiming at. He resurrects the spirit of the Palmach days by entering it once more. We should report 'adventures of various kinds, because nothing is more wonderful than an adventure whose constant movement precipitates the tremulous warm confrontation between curiosity and yearning'. The writers of the Palmach generation were writing for each other and for their times, replacing an immigrant with a native literature, conscious of being pioneers. But what is their position now? Can they change their voice?

There were those who did. No one was more universally associated with the State's early fiction than Moshe Shamir, who was as famous as Yizhar and more widely read. His stories were quite different, rich in action, whether in childhood reminiscence as in במו ידיו *Bemo Yadaw* (With His Own Hands) in sententious war tales such as הוא הלך בשדות *Hu Halakh basadoth* (He Walked in the Fields) or in historical epics such as מלך בשר ודם *Melekh Basar vadam* (King of Flesh and Blood, 1956) and כבשת הרש *Kivsath harash* (Lamb of the Pauper).

All these novels, however, whether set in the contemporary scene or in ancient times deal with policies, politics and statehood. Shamir recounted tales in which the characters' lives are intertwined with national events that shape them and are shaped by them, happily, heroically and, sometimes, tragically. But always the hero identifies with the body politic and is involved with it. But in 1966 Shamir wrote a novel called הגבול *Hagevul* (The Border), in which the hero, Raphael Orlan, is at odds with his Israeli ethos and attempts to break away. Orlan, who tells the story (for the most part), is in no-man's land beyond the Jerusalem border and strikes up an affair with a Scandinavian woman whose attraction lies in her being at liberty. She is not Israeli, therefore unrestricted in her travels as are Israelis. The Zionism that has created Israel is also castigated: 'Today Zionism has the smell of an airport, that mixture of cigar smoke and perfume'.

* * *

A similar mood is noted in other writers of the generation. Aharon Megged also wrote on national themes both in his short stories and in his novel חדווה ואני *Hedwah wa'ani* (Hedvah and I, 1954), which satirised a new tendency in Israeli society to reject the pioneering work of the founders of the State and to add to an unproductive bureaucracy. Such were the values of the new, small minded urban bourgeoisie. The author's irony implied a value system upholding the State's official ethos. But his novel החי על המת *Hahay 'al hameth* (Living on the Dead, 1965) portrays a character, Jonas, who feels he must reject that ethos in order to live an authentic existence. Jonas, a writer, is commissioned to devote a book to the Israeli pioneer Davidov, and is currently being sued for breach of contract. The writer comes to regard his subject as an enemy whose very presence is threatening. He would be totally rid of it: 'I don't want an enemy in my house ... I want to be my own master. I want to rest'.

Benjamin Tammuz, originally a writer of short stories about Tel Aviv childhood such as חולות הזהב *Holot Hazahav* (Golden Sands, 1950), similarly situates a character in a novel of the same period (actually the middle volume of a trilogy), בסוף מערב *Besof ma'arav* (At the Edge of the West, 1966).[1] This is another first-person account of a man, wounded in the War of Independence, who changes his job with great frequency. Although greatly gifted, his one ambition is to escape: 'I wanted to hide from the world'. He, too, has an affair with a girl from a Scandinavian embassy, Nora, and together they go to Spain. He had thought of Spain as a haven, but once there, the old historical associations for the Jew become real.

The theme of escape reappears in various novels of the period. לא מעכשיו לא מכאן *Lo me'akhshaw lo mikan* (Not of This Time, Not of This Place, 1963) by Yehuda Amichai, known primarily as a poet, is concerned with escape as is also היורד למעלה *Hayored lema'alah* (Descending Upward, 1961) by Yoram Kaniuk where the narrator finds himself alone in New York, a strange town. But the narrator loves the strangeness and embraces his own alienation. A slightly younger writer, Pinhas Sadeh, takes this loneliness for granted in his novel על מצבו של האדם *Al Matzavo Shel ha'adam* (The Human Condition, 1967). In his earlier writing he had already disclaimed interest in the merely national: 'The national war had no meaning for me and I could see nothing to fight for' in החיים כמשל *Hahayim kemashal* (Life as a Parable, 1957).

---

[1] Known in English translation as *A Castle in Spain* (Indianapolis, 1973).

* * *

There has been a change in direction and tone in the Israeli fiction of the 60s. Some writers who had made a reputation in earlier years, experimented in the 70s with 'new' forms, not necessarily rejecting national themes but giving them symbolic garb or composing tales that sound like allegories. Such is Tammuz's short novel הפרדס *Hapardes* (The Orchard, 1972), a fable treating the conflicting claims to the land on the part of Jews and Arabs. The word 'orchard' is not only a physical entity, but also (in hermeneutic terms) a mnemonic for the four methods of interpretation, and the secret world of the kabbalists. This approach is also suggested by the title of a later Tammuz novel, משלי הבקבוקים *Mishley habaqbuqim* (Parables of Bottles, 1979). Megged has become increasingly interested in sophisticated narrative techniques, as in החיים הקצרים *Haḥayim haqetzarim* (Short Life, 1972), where the banality of the plot, multiple adultery, is disguised by the irony of a narrative veil. The heroine here, a literary critic, questions the possibility of realism in the word, a possibility that this very novel represents. His three later works, על עצים ואבנים *Al etzim waavanim* (On Trees and Stones, 1973), מחברות אביתר *Maḥbroth Evyathar* (Eviatar's Notebooks, 1974) and העטלף *Ha'atalef* (The Bat, 1975) all deal in various ways with the themes of guilt and ambiguity, with identity and pseudo-identity (the cloak), with the confession and the irony of confession.

Literature can never be conveniently divided into generations, either thematically or stylistically. And certain literary approaches, thought to be archaic at one time, may well reppear later. But the type of moral allegory we have seen in the recent Israeli fiction of the middle generation is particularly favoured by the two most popular fiction writers of a younger generation—Abraham B. Yehoshua and Amos Oz. Yehoshua has thus far published mainly novellas, a genre that does not necessitate detailed social stratification in its makeup. The note of protest illustrated in terms of Sabra realism by Yizhar is taken up allegorically by Yehoshua in מול היערות *Mul haye'aroth* (Facing the Forests, 1968). An older, shortsighted student retreats to a forest where his function is to guard against the possibility of fire. He is studying the Crusader period. After making the acquaintance of the dumb Arab on the spot and learning of the existence of an Arab village buried beneath the Jewish forest, he himself is instrumental in setting the forest ablaze. Other stories of Yehoshua's are also a mélange of the real and the symbolic.

Oz writes both novels and short stories. In both he makes concentrated use of images which highlight the deep level of the story. He deals in extreme emotional states. His first volume of stories ארצות התן *Artzoth hathan* (Lands of the Jackal, 1965) conveys the howling of the jackal in the background. The jackal represents a threat; when Jerusalem is destroyed, it will be 'a habitation of jackals'. The heroine of the novel in מיכאל שלי *Mikhael Sheli* (My Michael, 1968) indulges in fantasies of rape and degradation which also bring 'cool pleasure'. And in the novel לגעת במיים לגעת ברוח *Laga'ath bamayim Laga'ath baruah* (Touch the water, Touch the wind, 1973) the themes of threat and Jewish destiny are woven together when the main characters, united in Israel, are submerged in a violent earthquake. The geological image is significant for Oz, as the earth's surface is liable to crack, whatever security it seems to offer. But also in his other stories the most powerful feeling evoked is the sense of danger.

A much less dramatic picture emerges from the work of Amalia Kahana-Carmon and Aharon Appelfeld. Kahana-Carmon is concerned with the subtle delineation of the intricacy of personal relationships, particularly as seen by the female partner involved. Appelfeld, who came to Israel as an adolescent, is less interested in individual psychology than in the fixity of relation between people, as determined by recent European history with its effect on the Jewish population. His stories (and, more recently, novellas and novels) are those of the survivor carefully etching the past as frozen into the present; the silhouette remains. A recent novella of his, however, באדנהיים עיר נופש *Badenhaym 'Ir Nofesh* (Badenheim, Holiday Resort) reproduced in the volume שנים ושעות *Shanim vesha'oth* (Years and Hours, 1975) experiments with a more flexible form. It portrays the changing shape of a spa community and its Jews, as Nazi policy gradually takes effect. The sense of decadence, perceptible to the reader but ignored by the participants, is reminiscent of Mann's *Death in Venice*.

* * *

VARIETIES OF REALISM IN CURRENT FICTION

The retreat from the explicit political still continues, although there has been a renewed interest in uncovering earliest historical roots in Israel amongst more established novelists such as Tammuz and Shamir. Writers have, naturally, not deviated in principle from their own idiosyncratic ways; the literary fabric cannot change. But their overt preoccupation has been with individual eccentricity. The 'I' juts out of his social context. And so, too, with younger writers. The waywardness of the individual, his (or her) obsessionalism, or his recollections and reconstructed role in the present, all, one way or another, seem to highlight his separateness. We will see how this expresses itself in the Israeli novels of the middle and late seventies.

Both Nathan Shaham in קירות עץ דקים *Qirot 'etz daqim* (Thin Partition, 1977) and Amos Oz in הר העצה הרעה *Har haetzah hara'ah* (The Hill of Evil Counsel, 1976) have produced collections of three novellas reflecting the recent historical and political situation of the Jews in Palestine and in the Diaspora. Oz's novellas are the closest of his opus to straight auto-biography, so far, told in a language sparer than usual. The first two items are related from the child's point of view, refracting events slightly beyond his youthful understanding, political and personal. The traditional Oz themes recur and extreme moods are perceived, but they are in large part bounced off a reality-bound consciousness. Although the title story itself is told in the third person in order to record events beyond the range of the child Hillel, Hillel is still often the implied narrator; his father is spoken of as 'daddy', even in indirect speech. But in spite of the naturalistic atmosphere established by the disciplined, semi-autobiographical stance, it is the dream that is pervasive. The dream of the child looking forward through the actions of others, and the recurrent dreams of the dying old man looking both backwards and forwards in longing, if not for himself and his beloved to whom he sends his letters, then for the nascent state which he will not live to see. The second story, אדון לוי 'Mr Levy', is a first-person childhood reflection on Jerusalem in the last stages of Mandatory rule. All is anticipation, as stated at the end: 'We must carry on waiting. What has been has been, and now there begins a new day'.

*
* *

But the Israeli novel is not always an amalgam of the social/collective/Jewish/Israeli sense, with the individual consciousness. We have also the exclusive concern with interpersonal relationships, in, for example, Varda Raziel Wiseltier's גבורים במלים *Giborim Bmillim* (Heroes in Words, 1977). It looks like a somewhat banal and trivial tale of successive and interlocking affairs and adulteries, where the (particularly female) emotions are protected from banality by declaring them banal. The total preoccupation of this novel is the erotic nature of the male-female relationship and its implications— boredom, satisfaction, adventure. Eventual defeat hovers over all the empty activities described to evoke out despair. Erotic emptiness seems also to be matched by a larger context of pointlessness in work, social, family and political life. Stimulation is immediate and casual. 'Satisfaction' is speedy but transient. All content is on the surface. It is a world of women who look to men. Sex exists in an erotic vacuum without much human or spiritual context. 'Connections' are indicated, but hardly realised The lack of a centre of gravity, or specific focus, is esplained by Ayalah: 'A circle has one centre ... but an ellipse two'. So why shouldn't her life have several foci? In addition to which she is looking for some project in which to sink herself, to surrender herself to completely. The sense of emptiness is grasped as well as the desperate clutching at invisible straws. For all the surface quality of the lives portrayed, there is no reluctance on the part of the dramatis personae to invoke grandiose notions such as 'love', 'purpose', 'fate', 'life' in an ever descending spiral of generalised terminology.

*
* *

Yotham Reuveny's book בעד ההזיה *Be'ad hahazayah* (For Fantasy, 1978) is, in spite of its title, more intimately related in its own texture to a type of reality. Pinhas Sadeh, in his introduction, considers the title, doubts that there is here a fantasy, or assumes that if there is, then perhaps it is God's fantasy, but concludes that maybe dream and reality are, in effect, one, and that 'we are such stuff as dreams are made on'. The author, in Sadeh's view, is dedicated to the proposition in this book that everything in life is holy, even the most unlikely, scurrilous material. There is religious meaning in, for example, man's condition (very much a Sadeh characterisation) in the toilet of the Tel-Aviv bus station. This book is in the line of Sadeh's own confessional writing, a type of Brennerist presentation, unfettered by the censorship of law, convention or disapproval. In such a passage, the writer puts night movements above daytime activities, night moments when space is allowed unlimited for the unbounded imagination, like, as he says, the monk who can experience the presence of God in his cell. He seeks to push aside the moment of waking and hide in his blankets. There is an authentic intensity in these confessions, phrased with a spare precision of language that constantly echoes itself. The sexual obsessionalism (homosexual) here is a concrete evocation of a mind trying to escape from its body. This is confessional writing with a minimum of external framework, plot or context. It is the confession of the half sleep, of the hazy awakening, of the recurrent, blurred fantasy. It is also a lament for the dream that will never materialise, or, to leap into the alternative terminology, for God who does not exist. In us, at any rate, 'Therefore will it be said, whispered and shouted: our Father, our King, God of our Gods, King of the King of Kings. Have mercy on us, answer us. For there is no God in us. And there is no green hope in us, only fear and doubt'. There is always the contrast between tranquillity (contentment) and that great impulse driving him back to the bus station. And then contentment will follow, perhaps exemplifying the words from Michaelangelo's thirty-seventh sonnet, 'In me la morte: in te la vita mia'. There will always exist a tension between these two poles, the waking reality and the quietude of the dream. But it seems that one necessitates the other. His greatest wish is to be what he has always wanted to be, that which can be fulfilled only at 'night', in the dream, which should carry no traces into the day. But there is also the nightmare, the experience of the threat to end the dream 'so that I should not spoil the routine of things'.

In these confessions, Reuveny sees himself as a witness, though paradoxically as a witness to matters unworthy of witness or record. His whole life is dedicated to the withdrawal from life. The writer must observe other lives and happenings. But why? A social loneliness becomes a necessary aloneness, an existential solitude. And this situation is the writer's subject. Is the material of any value? The writer is trying to make contact with the main point: 'Even if I do not succeed in putting down what seems to me if not contact with this main point, then at least an introduction to contact with the main point, a main point that cannot be visualised, although perhaps one could sense that a few pages, a particular section, are some sort of contact with the main point'. The narrator remembers his actual biography, and his need to rejoin those other I's. Again, the only refuge from the real world, which is also the world of trivia, is the night-time fantasy in 'the bolstered borders of the blanket'.

* * *

A novel of more conventional intent is Benjamin Tammuz's רקויאם לנעמן *Reqwiem lna'aman* (Requiem for Naaman, 1978), which, within a small compass, aspires to be not only a family saga covering the period from the first Aliyah (1881) until virtually the present day, but also thus a sort of history of Palestinian settlement. Here is a century of Jewish life, ideological as welling as chronological, revolving around the Yishuv. We have memories of Eastern Europe with the dream of the Holy Land, the longing for national redemption as against attachment to one's own local soil, and the contrast with Palestinian reality. The first lady in the family line of immigrants, Bella-Yaffa, is distraught at the longing realised, the wish made true, and the hope for Palestine become flesh and bones. She can only yearn for her own physical birthplace cursed by her father. Her alienation is the reverse of his. And she dies miserable in a drunken stupor, after being raped in the lonely waste by a passing Arab villager. Her son, Naaman, inherits her artistic temperament and ineffable longings. Two instincts are at war within the events and characters of the novel. One looks to strengthen its roots in the land, to recreate the ancient people of Palestine and to bring about national revival. The other is lyrical, personal and private. The novel represents a theatre of Zionist struggle and enactment within a family context. It is written in retrospect, bringing to bear on earlier episodes knowledge obtained later. Different temperaments derive from different parents; the life of art sits uneasily with the life of labour. The Naaman of the title is the archetypical devoted artist, removed from the concrete reality of the yishuv, whose detachment is signified by his almost total silence and his removal to Paris in pursuance of his music. There is also the ideological division between types of immi-

159

gration waves to Palestine, the individual farmers of the first and the collectivist agriculturalists of the second and third waves, represented in Tammuz's pleasantly modulated though somewhat contrived, literary language. The theme of the warring brothers, the Jacob-Esau refrain familiar in such novels as יעקב *Ya'aqov* (Jacob, 1971) and הפרדס *Hapardes* (The Orchard, 1972) with that glint of family ambiguities, is thus refracted again in a chronicle. The novel derives its unity through these diverse elements from the circular nature of the themes—the thread of the nature of Palestine and the thread of the family. These threads are drawn together through the person of Naaman, whose nature is investigated by his sister's grand-daughter. Temperamental affinities, like the names of the characters, recur in successive generations: public struggle and private will. But the question of unity must still be raised in the face of so many desperate elements. In the course of this short novel, the sense of Olympian detachment with which it had opened gets lost in political and social irony. Much is a rehearsal of well-known, public information, concentrating on recent history. But its total import aspires beyond that to a transcendent view of the issues raised and to a cyclical view of the family. As the young Bella-Yaffa says to a family meeting in 1974, 'They, those others, had a dream many years ago, and you are the fulfillment of that dream'.

Aharon Megged's novels also contain a large element of ambiguity. But that ambiguity usually devolves upon the identity of the individual (in most cases the central figure in the work), his history and motivation. עשהאל *Asahel* (Asahel, 1978) is no exception. Although the story is told by the central figure himself, his status remains the chief mystery. A very private person ascends the stage and there occupies the main refracting role. Everyone else's character bounces off Asahel. For this mystery to hold up, the narrator must be a mystery to himself. This specific technique requires and receives more idiomatic language than is usual in Megged's writing. But the book opens with an immediate problem: 'Strange things happen to me'. And the identity of the narrator is posed as problematic. Does he actually, concretely exist? 'I am amazed again and again how it happens that so often people don't see me at all. In spite of the fact that I am bulky enough and you could hardly call me invisible'. The narrator does not seem to be sufficiently established on the platform that he himself has erected. He attaches himself to the stage designer Aya and acts as her dogsbody, serving her in any way demanded. As he says, when playing down his own significance, 'Of the two of us, Aya is the really important one'. And in his relationship to the extrovert, self-confident Davidson, he is also practically non-existent. He melts in his own goodness towards the outside world, although he claims that evil seethes within. Why, otherwise, he asks, has he no friends? He is either anonymous or he appears in a strange guise. His mother, for example, mistakenly assumes him to be a poet. There are doubts, too, about his physical identity, particularly since the moment he fell off a donkey and fainted: 'When I recovered and opened my eyes to the heavens, I felt as though I were not myself but someone else'. This is an incident bearing recurrent reverberations, and he concludes the novel too with a description of that sensation of a vision of brightness. This was the source of his ill health and some physical incapacity. An earlier novel of Megged's העטלף *Ha'atalef* (The Bat, 1975) probes the issue of appearance and identity. A Jewish nationalist appears as a 'Jesuit' priest to the outside world. But whether his deep and his surface motivation are one and the same is not quite certain. Here, we are unsure of Asahel's status, whose ambiguity may stem from the fact that he was so close to death, 'as through I was already amongst the dead and was resurrected'. He prefers to dream rather than to work, and he constantly faces trouble with his employers in his rather lonely clerical job at the Statistical Office. As we see the events of the novel through his eyes, we are aware of the attitude of others to him. His mother wants him to be a poet, and even (as mentioned) pretends that he is such. Davidson is inexplicably hostile. Aya, to whom he is so attached, seems to indulge him with a pitying love. But her attitude to him too is difficult to grasp. Asahel reflects; 'Perhaps others want me to be different from what I am. But I won't change'. As he is insistent on his own integrity, so he would grant it to others. This is the only way not to hate. And hatred, too, makes you other than what you are. Asahel's chief effort then seems to be directed at acceptance of the world and its people as they are, and at the establishment of his own being. He both doubts his existence and also needs to bolster it. He imagines himself making a speech to Aya about the need for her to be herself, not to adapt to others for the sake of those others as well as for her own. The problem is that of identity. What, for example, is Aya's true nature? Is she such a saint in reality? Asahel, after his mother's death, ends up on the farm by himself, unresolved.

* * *

A very different picture is presented by Aharon Appelfeld, whose characters inhabit a twilight world of either the present dominated by a riveting, recent past which forces frozen attitudes, or of that past itself. His later work is bold in the staging of plot and character development within the dimensions of the novella. תור הפלאות *Tor Haplaot* (Period of Wonders, 1978) contains two novellas including the title story. Both involve recollection. The first (title) story is a first-person account set at the end of a summer, 1938, on a return home. The child narrator is accompanied by his mother. We have the familiar Appelfeld atmosphere—a decaying Europe, both physically and spiritually in an autumnal phase. Childhood is seen through an adult lens, and the decay is not only inevitable but even explicit. The story is a reflection of the gloom enveloping Europe and the disaster overtaking the Jews. People react variously to the crisis—ignoring it, accepting it, resenting it, fighting it—and we see a section of such reactions in this life fragment. This is an autogiographical type sketch set in early childhood, replete with the fears and fantasies of that period. Bourgeois, middle-European comfort cosseted the child, whilst a chill was blowing through the air. The child's point of view is not adopted exclusively, as when the narrator interposes, 'I didn't know then'. So the bitter anticipation can be transparent. As in that other of Appelfeld's recent works, 'Badenheim', we have a portrait of a dying civilisation, that very special creature which can be called 'Jewish Europe'. The contrast is indicated between the security and gaiety of a distant past and this final phase. The narrator's father, a well-known Viennese author, is pilloried for his decadence, so un-Austrian and for his unhealthy parasitism. This becomes a symbol of the Jew and his position in central Europe. His father is an adherent of Kafka, who is also associated with this particular Jewish condition. There seems to be internal hatred amongst the Jews, dislike of the bourgeois for the marginal artist and of the artist for the merchant. Both, ironically, are only incidentally attached to

Judaism, but in that momentous year (1938), they have become symptoms of it. The situation deteriorates as suddenly in the story as it did in historical fact, although the father persists in his contempt for all forms of overt Jewish expression. But, in whatever mysterious ways this occurs, the whole company is immediately set aside as Jewish in an 'Austrian' context. There is no explicit reference to Nazism, to the Anschluss, to politics—it is all there only in the utterances of the characters and in the knowledge of the reader. Of course, the narrator tells the story in retrospect, knowing the outcome. The father is exclusively immersed in his own efforts at self-rehabilitation. The rest of the family is taken away with the other Jews of the town to an 'unknown' destination, 'southwards'.

The second story, כללות הכל ולאחר שנים רבות *Kikhloth hakol uleaḥar shanim rabot*, is related from another perspective. We have noted that Appelfeld sets his stories either before the onslaught, in anticipation of it, or afterwards, when the characters bear the imprint of that dread period. But not in the heat of the event itself. This second story is transmitted by a narrator in the present, making a visit from his current home in Israel to the town of his birth. It is an attempt at rediscovery or recognition. Bruno has an ambivalent relationship to his city and its population, and to the surviving Jews. He is immediately repelled by the coarseness and ugliness of an orthodox train companion. The haze of the past seems sometimes very immediate, sometimes very cold. An emptiness pervades the place, though this is doubtless due to the particular lens of the observer, deraving that Jewish past. But then he says to himself that nothing has changed. Things are both unfamiliar and odd. The one man who seems familiar from those bygone days denies his identity. 'I am stunned at the abundance of well-known scenes', says Bruno to himself. This story is a late recollection of what constituted the background to the first tale. The story here is, from prelude to its sequel, disaster. But the recognition that our hero seeks is not granted. The whole territory is 'a familiar strange land', like Louise who used to live with his family and is now 'nothing but an old Austrian woman'. He also meets his cousin, illegitimate daughter of a reprobate uncle and a group of 'mixed' youths, with something of the Jew in them. Bruno's motivation is dubious, characterised by the hostile Brum as 'breathing out evil spirits'. That restlessness always accompanies Jewish presence is reiterated in the stories. Bruno's last act in the town is to strike the anti-Semitic Brum who so insults him. And the second story ends with an echo of the first. The train comes to take him away. There have been two exoduses from this same town. The first was the expulsion and end of the family and community, and then, decades later, the curtain is lowered on the scene of a revisitation. The recall of Agnon's אורח נטה ללון *Oreaḥ Natah lalun* (Guest for the Night, 1939), with the hero's visit back to his place of origin from Israel, is unavoidable. The Jew's roots are spread, even when the new soil is Israel, and the sidelong glance at the European Jew's fate is constantly made within the new State. As in his earlier autobiographical sketch כאישון העין *Keishon ha'ayin* (Like The Pupil of the Eye, 1972), Appelfeld seeks the roots and echoes of the contemporary Israeli Jew in another context. But autobiography is a different genre, conjuring up an actual, historical account of the narrator in the first person. It is still, though, an attempt in another medium to etch a Judaism dying in the old world, or as it is so characterised, 'an ancient tribe whose faith is lost and customs forgotten'.

Appelfeld's language has become in later works less meta-phorical and more 'prosaic'. The sentences tend to be more concrete, and the plot denser and quicker moving. 'At the end of April Bruno returned to his city, the city where he was born. The train from Vienna to Schtelheim was packed', opens the story ככלות הכל ולאחר שנים רבות *Kikhlot Hakol*. Whereas the autobiography opens, 'Upraised, exalted, worshipped, rustled the ancient words, hanging and sinking'. This may indicate a greater confidence on the part of the author in the stark presentation of narrative, without contrived impregnation of atmosphere. But there are still traces of the familiar mingling of the concrete with the abstract, the odd, concretising image. The seasons still cling to the plot, indicating its tempo and mood. There is more dialogue and external action. The story is left more to itself, creating an effect of economy rather than strain.

Amaliah Kahana-Carmon's triptych שדות מגנטיים *Sadoth Magnetiyim* (Magnetic Fields, 1977) is concerned with the nature of the link between people, particularly the attraction between men and women. This attraction does not necessarily nor even usually lead to satisfactory fulfillment. Firstly, because emotions are not constant, and secondly, because they are not replicated in each other in parallel waves. There is a moment of splendour sensed by one party, unpredictably and arbitrarily. The other party may be unaware of the sensation generated. But then this moment can fade away irrevocably, and only the memory linger to be recorded. The 'magnetic fields' of the title indicate the particular range of the individual's pathos. The metaphor suggests the impossibility of transcendence; the object magnetised cannot, after all, wander from its own field. Neither can an object/person move into another field unless the primary field is demagnetised, i.e. neutralised. Carmon's writing does not provide an explanation of the sensation, nor of its movement. It rather charts its progress.

The first short section describes the contact between a United Nations officer and a thirteen-year old Israeli girl. Shoshana, on the bus trip where they meet, is already deeply 'in love' with him, 'For him I no longer belong to Israel, but to the UN'. But she interprets his sexual advances as violence. Her emotions are inexplicable, her attachment puzzling. She has asked herself what it is that has cut into her and consumed her so. There is no answer, but 'she feels herself destroyed, not knowing anything'. They part after the journey. This brief acquaintanceship has not even furnished her with knowledge of his name, and she cannot speak his language. But she is totally transformed and will never be the same again. The moment of ecstasy, however, is interspersed with the reality of the everyday. Her normality is that of the family routine. The two levels exist side by side, and she tries to recapture that glorious moment: 'Hunting again what has gone and is now only delight, all delight. Though there are preserved within it the fullness of its lost taste and depth of colours—sharply, like a fist on the jaw'.

The main section of the triptych, שם חדר החדשות *Sham hadar hahadashot*, deploys concentrated prose in order to conjure up a more sustained obsession of (this time) a man for a woman. In Carmon's stories, whether first or third person accounts, we are presented with a single point of view. The main object of the writing is to indicate the lack of mutuality in the encounter. This long story tells of an intense, inexplicable attachment that, in all, extended over a matter of weeks. A middle-aged Israeli dramatist staying in a London hostel meets up with an American girl Wendy, and becomes totally besotten with her. This period is recalled a year later by a 'brain' which, says the narrator, cannot absorb any new experiences because of the intensity of this one. Their first encounter, prosaic at the breakfast table, is shrouded in mystery. What exactly happens when two people meet? Not only of opposite sexes, but even when they are of the same sex? Two women for example; 'Women getting to know each other I always find intangible. Something of the type—shoes in a drawer, footless. What are the various ways of passing dead time?' His attitude to her is unstable, not of a piece. What he seeks out more than anything is 'the most important thing in life for him—people. But not just the fact of people. Rather, their significance'. He has, he discovers, 'an all-consuming desire to see people as being of significance'. And to this end, all else is sacrificed. To the need 'to be attached in my heart to another without restraint, wildly, dependently'. To such a degree does the obsession rage that he asks himself whether the whole encounter was worthwhile: 'Now that I reconstruct it, I have a question. Am I sorry or glad that I know her? Answer: I have gained information'. This is the author's technique for reducing the voltage in such a highly-charged context. When the concern of the novel is so intensely subjective, so exclusively related to feelings, a quasi-scientific measure is imported. So, although the material is personal, the writing can be objective, neutrally recording. This accounts for the author's reverence for the particular, the specific, the everyday, the lists of items, the sense of routine. These things serve both to pin the event in a context of recognised, naturalistic reality, and also to highlight the splendour of the emotion, the central concern, as defined here, for example, by the narrative voice. But there is also the contrast in the receiving party, in this case Wendy, who fails to find herself on the same wavelength, or even, to use the cliche, inhabiting the same universe of discourse. For the narrator Zevulun, the encounter has been awesome, revitalising, startling. He writes to her, 'I am a person no longer young ... and you have been my swan song. Now I can only thank heaven for that grace, that it happened once more. After so many years. After I had forgotten the meaning of what matters'. But Wendy's response locates the isolation of those in contact: 'You assume that our friendship embraced a layer of closeness, which ... in effect, existed only in your mind'. She concentrates on the point of what each one is and does 'separately'. There is disjunction and parting. We are all in different magnetic fields. But the writing is a recollection and a memorial. Goethe's 'Elective Affinities' are reversed.

* * *

One thing that does emerge from the foregoing discussion is the inadequacy of the term 'realism' in itself to classify fictional writing. 'Realism' can mean precisely recorded detail of class behaviour, as with Flaubert, or the attempted exclusion of the 'point of view' to make the writing objective, as in the 'nouveau roman'. Or it might be neither of these, but some other imitation of some aspect of reality. Unless accompanied by a qualifier, the word is virtually meaningless. Any literary work must be to a degree 'realistic' in that it uses a communicating language, and draws the reader into a communicated world. But is 'realism' a mimicry of a type of social reality, à la Wiseltier, which does not satisfactorily grasp that reality? Or could it even be such material whose explicit aspiration is directed elsewhere, as in Reuveni's work? Is it merely the introduction of historical material as a background for the recorded chronology of a family, as in Tammuz's novel? Or the attempt to come to terms, with the past in the present, as we have with Appelfeld? Megged's heroes may be both strange and real. Kahana-Carmon, for all the specialness of the recorded consciousness in her work, is representing an event, at least in the mind of her heroes and heroines. Is the mixture of naturalism and allegory found fluctuating in both Oz and Yehoshua also 'realistic'? In like case is the conscription of the term 'naturalism', an attempted terminological refinement which cannot grasp nor suggest the divergence of typologies in any segment of fictional efforts by different hands. Even this limited selection of recent Israeli fiction would defy such categorisation. A proper description has to take into account the particular aspiration and texture of the opus in order to describe and appraise its nature and achievement.

RECENT NOVELS OF AMOS OZ AND A.B. YEHOSHUA

A frequent phenomenon in the historiography of modern Hebrew literature is the yoking of two writers together so that they form a pair, sometimes reluctant, sometimes illmatched, sometimes uneven in talent and sometimes coupled at random.

In the case of Oz and Yehoshua though, there is a coincidence of circumstance, talent and creativity. Both started writing Hebrew fiction in the mid 60s. Both initially hailed from Jerusalem and then left — Oz for a kibbutz and Yehoshua for Haifa. More importantly, both looked for new ways making a statement within the secular tradition of Hebrew fiction whilst seeking the essence of the modern Israeli situation. Both have sought a broad canvas to describe modern Israeli man in a world of tension, threat and historical ambiguity. Both employ strong plot lines and depth psychology to create effects of surprise and undermine the reader's determined expectations.

Both writers also produced novels in 1982, in both cases breaking fairly long fictional silence. And as they are two of Israeli's outstanding novelists, their work has been eagerly awaited and snatched up by an ardent readership. But both novels have been long in gestation, so that their origins go back well into the 70s. Four chapters of Oz's *Menuḥah nekhonah* (A Perfect Peace) were published as a separate entity in 1970, and those are the chapters that set the tone. Yehoshua's *Gerushim Meuḥarim* (Late Divorce) was commenced on 1978. Both explore the psychology of the individual — Oz within the framework of the collective, the kibbutz, Yehoshua within the framework of an enlarged family, three generations with their attachments and loyalties.

Oz's is a kibbutz novel in the simple sense that it is set in a kibbutz. Whether this bare fact is sufficient to place it within a special genre of kibbutz writing is another question. Oz acknowledges his debt to an earlier kibbutz novelist, David Malz, whose work *Hasha'ar na'ul* (The Gate is Closed) appeared in 1959. There are many other stories and novels with a kibbutz setting, by, amongst others, Z. Luz and N. Frankel. But the most obvious lead to *Menukhah nekhonah* is Oz's own earlier *Maqom aḥer* (Another Place, 1966). In the new novel, we are presented with two (psychological) facts — 1) That Yonatan Lipschitz, born and bred on the kibbutz, wants to leave, and 2) That Azariah Gitlin, originally from the Diaspora (country unspecified but probably Russia), more recently a rootless wanderer in Israel, wants to settle on the kibbutz. These intertwined motives constitute the focus of the whole. The reader is led to expect a substitution of roles, the displacement of each by the other. Each has something that the other wants but that he himself earnestly and passionately rejects. In

Yonatan's case, it is rootedness in a routine life devoted to Israel within the framework of Israeli socialism. In Azariah's case, it is precisely the opposite — homelessness, lack of frame-work and absence of a base for progressive Jewish self-determination. The book then suggests the variety of human motivation within a dialectical pattern of opposites. It is a game of musical chairs for two, with satisfaction guaranteed by the exchange of places. Or is it? Can Azariah's need be so easily satisfied or is there a restlessness moving beyond the suggested parameters of kibbutz life? Will Yonatan's need to be unfet-tered by the local and predictable expectations of kibbutz life be satisfied by an undefined trip beyond? The questions are not necessarily answered. Indeed, one of the weaknesses of the work is the apparent arbitrariness of the denouement and ending. But certainly, this is a novel about psychological need, yearning, framework, dissatisfaction, ambition and social fabric — and happens to be set in a kibbutz. Other novels are set in villages, towns or farms. This does not necessarily imply a generic category.

The parallel with Oz's earlier *Maqom aher* derives not solely from the setting. There is a paramount atmosphere of threat, inexplicable attraction and indifference, the manipulation of fates from a distance by others who once had a connection with the kibbutz. Although the plot of both novels is mostly conveyed by an omniscient narrator, occasionally a first person plural voice explicitly intervenes to comment. Suddenly the word "we" comes up. And this "we" is the collective represen-tation of the kibbutz, the expression of that society. Yonatan is set against the background of that society. The fact that he needs to leave is an index of his rejection of the consensus. He has been reared on the certain, powerful ideology of his politically influential, ideological father. But the son does not trust that voice. When his father talks of 'historical meaning' or of the 'obligations of youth' in that sure, morally demanding tone, Yonatan freezes up. "He was a quiet man. He neither liked words nor trusted them." The kibbutz has a sense of its own significant place in history. But the outsider, whether already outside, as here the rival of Yonatan's father (and perhaps his actual biological father?) living the life of a great financial magnate in America, or the potential outsider, like Yonatan, is a threat. For the narrator in *Maqom aher*, the place of the kibbutz is guaranteed not only by will and ideology, but by the very structure of the earth's surface which sets Israel off from Syria. This certainty of one's historical course can be so easily undermined and it is constantly under threat. It is under threat — sexually from strange (i.e. unorthodox) bondings, socially — from attempts to attract the family beyond the kibbutz boundaries (matched by the parallel inclination of Yonatan), politically — from the decline of old-style ideology. We seem to be at the crossroads, with all the signs now pointing away from the direction of that veteran Israel. Yonatan's father is fading. Physically, he has suffered from a stroke, and his son has abandoned not only him but everything that he has built up and valued. His wife is consumed with hatred and resentment (there are always echoes of that mysterious association many years ago). Is this the novel of the system's demise? If Oz has told stories of ambiguous threat and fear, these elements can now be actualised. But no. Suddenly everything seems to return to normal. For no apparent reason, Yonatan comes back. The counter challenge from America is dropped. Yonatan's mother is reconciled to the situation, and is even tender to her sick husband. Srolick, the old associate of Yonatan's father, so sane and balanced, now the kibbutz secretary, sums up in his notebooks: "There are two or three things that can be done. So they must be done." Whatever the freedom of action, whatever the instincts, dormant or active, in some way that history has reasserted itself. This does not mean that life simply returns to normal. The *status quo ante* contains additional elements. Yonatan now lives again with his wife Rimona, but Azariah remains, too. The unorthodox threesome is absorbed into the resumed pattern of the kibbutz.

Questions are inevitably and perhaps deliberately left open by the author. We are not quite certain of the narrator or at least of the narrative tone, whether it be ironic, critical or neutral. As in other of Oz's stories, the female is mysterious. Even in *Mikhael sheli* (My Michael, 1968), when the woman Hannah was the narrator, her motivation and aspirations were unfathomable. There she was dominant, the tone setter, the aggressor. Here, Rimona, Yonatan's wife, is a figure in the story — passive, accepting, lovely, regarded by others as simple. But in general for the author (narrator/s), motivation or cause are very suspect entities. We do not know exactly why one person wants to leave the kibbutz, why another wants to come, why the first person returns. We are left with the rather unsatisfactory ending (not a conclusion) that things go on. The title, taken from the "El male rahamim" prayer,[2] expresses what Srolick would like to find in death but fears will not come. The germs of many ideas are left undeveloped. Relationships are illustrated interestingly, but then dropped at the critical moment. And the startling potential of the kernel situation is not here realized.

Just as one might raise the question of whether Oz's novel is in the kibbutz genre, one could also ask whether Yehoshua's novel is in the family genre. Certainly, its concern is with one family, with the relationships within it and those springing from its members. Until the writing of *Hameahev* (The Lover, 1978), Yehoshua had favoured the long story/novella as an instrument to bring out the psychological ambiguities of his main characters. The difficulty that the author had with that particular framework lay in this narrative perspective. Sometimes, the narrator was inside the event, sometimes on the outside, commenting. But this rather unsatisfactory amalgam produced an uncontrolled ambiguity undermining narrative credibility. Yehoshua solved this particular problem in *Hameahev* by allowing his characters (in a technique derived from Faulkner) to relate the story from their own point of view, endowing the total with a multiple focus, removing the ambiguity of narrator and sharpening comment. Apparently the technique proved sufficiently satisfactory for it to be readopted in the current work. Each participant in this family story takes up the narrative from the point left off by the previous narrator to continue the story from his own viewpoint. But again, in the discussion of genres, the familial framework is an instrument for the analysis of how individuals relate to that structure and how they view themselves.

The novel's central event is the return of the 66-year old Yehuda from America to Israel to try to finalise his divorce. He thus visits his institutionalised wife, but he also has to go to his daughter's family in Haifa, to his younger son Assa, who lives with his beautiful wife in Jerusalem, and he also meets up with his other son, Zvi, who lives in Tel Aviv. Only the Haifa couple have children, the older of whom, Gadi, also relates part of the story. So we see his parents and grandfather through his eyes, too. This apparently very commonplace family structure con-

[2] Recited in the course of the "Yizkor" memorial service on major festivals.

ceals a hive of irregularities. Zvi is a homosexual undergoing analysis and out to make his fortune from the impending divorce. Anna seems driven by his own impotence into career ambitiousness and a passsionate dramatisation of the terrorism that he teaches. Assa's wife retreats into literary and narcissistic fantasies. The eldest child in Haifa seems the sanest and most contented member of the family, but she is totally dominated by her lawyer husband, known as the "clown," whose tongue is totally uncontrolled as he pursues his own fantasies (e.g. freeing a client whom he believes to be a murderer) in an excess of babble.

The projected divorce is the catalyst for an expression of all these ambiguities, paricularly as they focus on the father (grandfather) and his divorce. Is the divorce really desired and, if so, why? Did his wife once seriously try to kill him? These questions, left unanswered, lurk in the background. Divorce is not a neutral fact, but a further link in the chain broken, a breach of the circle. The family is separated off into segments of partial and different interest, but they nevertheless share a point of convergence. As a circle they have a centre, which, here, is the father, Yehuda. The unsatisfactory relationship between the father and his two sons, Zvi and Assa, has determined their respective relationships and also the nature of their attempted reconciliation. The events take place over the few days of Yehuda's visit to Israel, and climaxes on the first day of Pesach, particularly when the family is all invited by Zvi's aging boyfriend, Raphael Calderon, to a festive dinner in a quality restaurant. The movement of attitude to Yehuda is from resentment (at his selfishness, neglect, divorce) to acceptance and even nostalgia. He begins to feel that he will be missed by the others. If the family is a complete circle, his movement out by divorce, surrender of his flat, return (this time permanent) to America, will ultimately impair that circle. This family dinner is the cantata of the attemped reconciliation, an effusion of renewed possibilities. When Yehuda is informed by Zvi that he will be missed, he says: "My cheeks were on fire, my insides turned over." Calderon's invitation had been issued in "incomprehensible excitement." The meal turned, in the words of the "clown," into a "divorce celebration." But then suddenly, this new unity, the sense of dance, begins to fall apart. Yehuda notes discord. Assa and his wife had not been speaking to each other. Zvi and Assa seem to be involved in very intense separate discussions. And then it is revealed (by Calderon) that Zvi intends to sell the house which Yehuda has just made over to his wife. The children inexplicably begin to cry and force the breakup of the party — they apparently sense the disintegration. So Yehuda returns to his wife's institution and steals back the papers making over the home to his wife. And in one of the paradoxical conclusion so beloved of Yehoshua, Yehuda, who has acted as the pivot of the story and who relates the final section, gets caught up (literally and metaphorically) in his visit to the hospital. He tries on his wife's clothes and cannot then extricate himself from them. Naturally, others think that he is mad. Is he? Has he substituted himself for his wife Naomi (the stange powerful porter seems to call him that)? Or has he so identified himself with the place that he cannot move away? Is this his way of retaining the family circle?

In both novels, we have a circular movement. In *Menuḥah nekhonah*, Yonatan leaves the kibbutz only to return to a rather changed situation. In *Gerushim meuḥarim*, Yehuda comes to his family to try to effect a permanent breach but is then left ambiguously *in situ*.[3] Yehoshua's novel concludes under concrete threat. The porter seems to be about to kill him: 'Suddenly you are in terrible straits!" Oz's novel concludes more tentatively with a gesture towards the 'perfect peace' that will likely evade us. The action in the Yehoshua novel springs more genuinely from the circumstances delineated and developed within a controlled, analysed and realistic vein. Although the surreal emerges at the end, it is charged and guaranteed by the preceding account. The Oz story, although in some ways more attractively written, lacks that cogency.

Both novels are of individuals and relationships within different settings. But although the backdrop is characteristically Israeli, in both cases we witness a further movement away from overt State concerns. Here is the new Israeli fiction without the obvious Israeli concomitant ingredients; the fiction of the Israeli person, in his social context.

---

[3] It should be clear from an outline of the plot and of the terminology used that this novel can also be read as an allegory of the ambivalent relationship between the Jews and Israel, culminating in an attempted divorce. But not all pieces of the allegorical jigsaw fit consistently into this scheme.

BIBLIOGRAPHY

WORKS IN HEBREW

Agnon, S.Y., והיה העקוב למישור (*Vehaya he'aqov lemishor*, 1912) in
אלו ואלו (*Elu wa'elu*, Tel-Aviv, 1949); הכנסת כלה (*Hakhnasat
kalah*, Tel-Aviv, 1931); אורח נטה ללון (*Oreah natah lalun*, Tel-
Aviv, 1939).

Amichai, Y., לא מעכשיו לא מכאן (*Lo me'akhshaw lo mikan*, Tel-Aviv,
1963).

Appelfeld, A., אדני הנהר (*Adney hanahar*, Tel-Aviv, 1971); העור
והכתנת (*Ha'or wehakuthonet*, Tel-Aviv, 1971); כאישון העין (*Keishon
ha'ayin*, Tel-Aviv, 1972); שנים ושעות (*Shanim wesha'ot*, Tel-Aviv,
1975); תור הפלאות (*Tur haplaot*, Tel-Aviv, 1978).

Ben Amotz, D., לא שם זין (*Lo sam zayin*, Tel-Aviv, 1973).

Burla, Y., אשתו השנואה (*Ishto hasnuah*, Tel-Aviv, 1920); בלי כוכב (*Beli
kokhav*, Tel-Aviv, 1920); נפתולי אדם (*Naftuley adam*, Tel-Aviv,
1929); עלילות עקביה (*'Aliloth 'aqavyah*, Tel-Aviv, 1939); בעל בעמיו
(*Ba'al be'amaw*, Tel-Aviv, 1962).

Gouri, H., הספר המשוגע (*Hasefer hameshuga'*, Tel-Aviv, 1971).

Hareven, S., עיר ימים רבים (*'Ir yamim rabim*, Tel-Aviv, 1973).

Hazaz, H., בקץ הימים (*Beqetz hayamim*, Tel-Aviv, 1935); ריחיים שבורים
(*Rehayim shevurim*, Tel-Aviv, 1942); חיושבת בגנים (*Hayoshevet
baganim*, Tel- Aviv, 1944); אבנים רותחות (*Avanim rotehot*, Tel-
Aviv, 1946); דלתות נחושת (*Dalthoth nehosheth*, Tel-Aviv, 1957);
בקולר אחד (*Beqolar ehad*, Tel-Aviv, 1963).

Horowitz, M., קרקס הפרעושים (*Qirqas hapar'oshim*, Tel-Aviv, 1977).

Kahana-Carmon, A., בכפיפה אחת (*Bikhfifah ahat*, Tel-Aviv, 1966);
וירח בעמק אילון *Weyareah be'emeq ayalon*, Tel-Aviv, 1971); שדות
מגנטיים (*Sadoth magnetiyim*, Tel-Aviv, 1977).

Kaniuk, Y., היורד למעלה (*Hayored lma'alah*, Tel-Aviv, 1961).

Megged, A., חדוה ואני (*Hedwah waani*, Tel-Aviv, 1954); החי על המת
(*Hahay 'al hamet*, Tel Aviv, 1965); החיים הקצרים (*Hahayim
haqtzarim*, Tel-Aviv, 1972); על עצים ואבנים (*'Al etzim waavanim*,
Tel-Aviv, 1973); מחברות אביתר (*Mahbaroth evyathar*, Tel-Aviv,
1974); העטלף (*Ha'atalef*, Tel-Aviv, 1975); עשהאל (*'Asahel*, Tel-
Aviv, 1978).

Michael, S., שוים ושוים יותר (*Shawim weshawim yoter*, Tel-Aviv, 1974);
חסות (*Hasut*, Tel-Aviv, 1977).

Mosinsohn, I., בערבות הנגב (*Be'arvot hanegev*, Tel-Aviv, 1949).

Orpaz, Y., עור בעד עור (*'Or be'ad 'or*, Tel-Aviv, 1963); מות ליסנדה (*Mot
Lisanda*, Tel-Aviv, 1966); נמלים (*Nemalim*, Tel-Aviv, 1968);
מסע דניאל (*Masa' daniel*, Tel-Aviv, 1969).

Oz, A., ארצות התן (*Artzoth hatan*, Tel-Aviv, 1965); מקום אחר (*Maqom aher*, Tel-Aviv, 1966); מיכאל שלי (*Mikhael sheli*, Tel-Aviv, 1968); עד מוות (*'Ad mawet*, Tel-Aviv, 1971); ארבעה פרקים ראשונים (*Arba'ah praqim rishonim*, Tel-Aviv, 1972); לגעת במים לגעת ברוח (*Laga'at bamayim laga'ath baruah*, Tel-Aviv, 1973); הר העצה הרעה (*Har ha'etza hara'ah*, Tel-Aviv, 1976); מנוחה נכונה (*Menuhah Nekhonah*, Tel-Aviv, 1982).

Reuveni, Y., בעד ההזיה (*Be'ad hahazaya*, Tel-Aviv, 1978).

Sadeh, P., החיים כמשל (*Hahayim kmashal*, Tel-Aviv, 1958); על מצבו של האדם (*'Al matzavo shel haadam*, Tel-Aviv, 1967).

Shabtai, Y., הדוד פרץ ממריא (*Hadod peretz mamri*, Tel-Aviv, 1972); זכרון דברים (*Zikhron dvarim*, Tel-Aviv, 1977).

Shaham, N., הלוך ושוב (*Halokh washow*, Tel-Aviv, 1972); קירות עץ דקים (*Qirot 'etz daqim*, Tel-Aviv, 1977).

Shamir, M., הוא הלך בשדות (*Hu halakh basadot*, Tel-Aviv, 1947); תחת השמש (*Tahat hashamesh*, Tel-Aviv, 1950); במו ידיו (*Bemo yadaw*, Tel-Aviv, 1951).; מלך בשר ודם (*Melekh basar wadam*, Tel-Aviv, 1954); כבשת הרש (*Kivsat harash*, Tel-Aviv, 1957); הגבול (*Hagvul*, Tel-Aviv, 1966); חיי עם ישמעאל (*Hayay 'im yishmael*, Tel-Aviv, 1968); יונה מחצר זרה (*Yonah mehatzer zarah*, Tel-Aviv, 1973).

Tammuz, B., חולות הזהב (*Holoth hazahav*, Tel-Aviv, 1950); בסוף מערב (*Besof ma'arav*, Tel-Aviv, 1966); יעקב (*Ya'aqov*, Tel-Aviv, 1971); הפרדס (*Hapardes*, Tel-Aviv, 1972); רקויאם לנעמן (*Reqwiem lna'aman*, Tel-Aviv, 1978.

Wiseltier, V., Rasiel, גבורים במלים (*Giborim bmilim*, Tel-Aviv, 1977).

Yehoshua, A.B., מול היערות (*Mul haye'arot*, Tel-Aviv, 1968); בתחלת קיץ 1970 (*Bitehilat qayitz '70*, Tel-Aviv, 1972); המאהב (*Hameahev*, Tel-Aviv, 1977); גרושים מאוחרים (*Gerushim meuharim*, Tel-Aviv, 1982).

Yizhar, S., ארבעה סיפורים (*Arba'ah sipurim*, Tel-Aviv, 1950); ימי צקלג (*Yemey tziqlag*, Tel-Aviv, 1958); ספורי מישור (*Sipurey mishor*, Tel-Aviv, 1964).

ENGLISH TRANSLATIONS OF WORKS CITED TOGETHER
WITH OTHER WORKS BY THE SAME AUTHOR
(* — a collection of stories)

Agnon, Samuel Joseph, *In the heart of the sea; a story of a journey to the land of Israel.* (New York: Schocken, 1947; London: Gollancz, 1967), tr. Israel M. Lask; *The Bridal Canopy.* (Garden City: Doubleday, Doran, 1937, 1967 and London: Gollancz, 1968), tr. Israel M. Lask; *A guest for the night.* (London: Gollancz, 1968, New York: Schocken, 1968), tr. Misha Louvish; *Twenty-one stories.* (New York: Schocken and London: Gollancz, 1970, various translators, ed. Nahum N. Glatzer; *Betrothed, and Edo and Enam: two tales.* (New York: Schocken and London: Gollancz, 1966, also Harmondsworth: Penguin, 1971), tr. Walter Lever.

Amichai, Yehuda, *Not of this time, not of this place.* (New York: Harper and Row, 1968 and London: Vallentine-Mitchell, 1973), tr. Shlomo Katz.

Appelfeld, Aharon, * *In the wilderness: stories.* (Jerusalem: Akshav Publishing House, 1965), pp. 199. By various translators. *Badenheim 1939.* (Boston, Godine, 1980, pp. 148, also London: Dent, 1981), pp. 160. *The age of wonders.* (Boston, Godine, 1981), pp. 270. Dalya Bilu.

Ben-Amotz, Dahn, *To remember, to forget.* (Philadelphia: Jewish publication Society of America, 1973), pp. 399. Zeva Shapiro.

Burla, Yehuda, *In darkness striving.* (Jerusalem: Institute for the translation of Hebrew literature, Israel Universities Press, 1968), pp. 135. Joseph Shachter.

Gouri, Haim, *The chocolate deal.* (New York, Holt, Rinehart and Winston, 1968), pp. 141. Seymour Simckes.

Hareven, Shulamith, *City of many days.* (Garden City: Doubleday, 1977), pp. 207. Hillel Halkin.

Hazaz, Haim, *Mori Sa'id.* (New York, Abelard-Schuman, 1956, pp. 340) Ben Halpern. *Gates of bronze.* (Philadelphia: Jewish Publication Society of America, 1975, xxiii, pp. 400). S. Gershon Levi.

Kaniuk, Yoram, *The Acrophile.* (New York: Atheneum, 1961), pp. 182. Zeya Shapiro. *Himmo, king of Jerusalem.* (New York: Atheneum; London: Chatto and Windus, 1962), pp. 246. Joseph Shachter. *Adam resurrected.* (New York, Atheneum, 1971; London: Chatto and Windus, 1972), pp. 370. Seymour Simckes. *Rocking horse.* (New York: Harper and Row, 1977), pp. 408.

Richard Flantz. *The story of Aunt Shlomzien the Great.* (New York: Harper and Row, 1978), pp. 171. Zeva Shapiro.

Megged, Aharon, *Fortunes of a fool.* (London, Gollancz; New York: Random House, 1962), pp. 304. Aubrey Hodes. *The living on the dead.* (London, J. Cape, 1970), pp. 251. Misha Louvish. *The short life.* (New York, Taplinger Publishing Co., 1980), pp. 278. Miriam Arad.

Mossinsohn, Igai, *Judas.* (New York, St. Martin's Press, 1963), pp. 305. Jules Harlow.

Orpaz, Yithak, *The death of Lysanda.* (London, J. Cape, 1970), pp. 110. Richard Flint [= Flantz].

Oz, Amos, *My Michael.* (London: Chatto and Windus; New York: Knopf, vi, London: Fontana, 1975), pp. 224. Nicholas de Lange. *Elsewhere perhaps.* (New York: Harcourt, Brace, Jovanovich, 1973; London: Secker and Warburg, 1974; New York, Penguin Press, 1979), pp. 288. Nicholas de Lange. *Touch the water, toutch the wind.* (New York: Harcourt, Brace. Jovanovich, 1974; London: Chatto and Windus, 1975; London, Fontana, 1976), pp. 179. Nicholas de Lange. *Unto death.* (New York: Harcourt, Brace, Jovanovich, 1975), pp. 166. Includes 2 stories "Crusade" and "Late love". Nicholas de Lange. * *The hill of evil counsel.* (New York, Harcourt, Brace, Jovanovich; London: Chatto and Windus, 1978; London: Fontana, 1980), pp. 210. Nicholas de Lange. *Soumchi.* (New York; Harper and Row; London: Chatto and Windus, 1981), pp. 89. Penelope Farmer. * *Where the jackals howl, and other stories.* (New York: Harcourt, Javanovich; London: Chatto and Windus, 1981), pp. 217. Nicholas de Lange. *In the land of Israel* (London: Chatto and Windus, 1984).

Sadeh, Pinhas, *Life as a parable.* (London: A. Blond, 1966, pp. 368). Richard Flantz.

Shamir, Moshe, *The king of flesh and blood.* (New York: Vanguard Press: London, East and West Library, 1958), pp. 542. David Patterson. *He walked through the fields.* (Jerusalem: World Zionist Organization, Dept. for Education and Culture in the Diaspora, 1959, pp. 72. Aubrey Hodes. *The fifth Wheel.* (London: Bodley Head, 1971), pp. 128. Aubrey Hodes. *David's stranger* (New York: Abelard-Schuman, 1965), pp. 219. Re-issued under the title *The Hittite must die.* (New York: East and West Library, 1978). *With his own hands.* (Jerusalem: Institute for the translation of Hebrew Literature, Israel Universities Press, 1970), xi, pp. 253. Joseph Schachter.

Tammuz, Benjamin, *Castle in Spain.* (Indianapolis: Bobbs-Merrill, 1973; London: Gollancz, 1974), pp. 311. Joseph Shachter. *Minotaur.* (New York, New American Library, 1981, pp. 210). Kim Parfitt, Mildred Budney. * *A rare cure.* (Tel-Aviv, Hakibbutz

Hameuchad, Institute for the translation of Hebrew Literature, 1981), pp. 216. Joseph Shachter. *Requiem for Naaman.* (New York, New American Library, 1982), pp. 228. Mildred Budny, Yehuda Safran.

Yehoshua, Avraham B., * *Three days and a child.* (New York: Doubleday, 1970; London: P. Owen, 1971), pp. 260. Miriam Arad. * *Early in the summer of 1970.* (Two stories translated by Miriam Arad and one by Pauline Shrier). (Garden City: Doubleday, 1977; London: Heinemann, 1980), pp. 165. *The lover.* (Garden City: Doubleday, 1978), pp. 352. Philip Simpson.

Yizhar, S., * *Midnight convoy, and other stories.* (Jerusalem: Institite for the translation of Hebrew literature, Israel Universities Press, 1969), pp. 273. Misha Louvish, Miriam Arad, Reuven Ben-Yosef.

INDEX

ORIENTALISTE, P.B. 41, B-3000 Leuven